GTP

THE GHOST TEAM PROJECT
www.theghostteam.com

Designed by HousSam Mouazin
Translations and adaptations by Studio ADAD, Milan
info@adadonline.com

❈

Original title in Italian edition: *Napoleone il Comunicatore*
Copyright © 2012 by Egea S.p.A. – All rights reserved –
egea.edizioni@unibocconi.it – www.egeaonline.it

❈

Due to the nature of Internet, the Editor disclaims responsibility
for any eventual change of address or in format of the aforementioned site.

First edition 2019

ISBN 978-1532917523

In accordance with company policy, this volume has been
produced on paper obtained from trees grown in sustainable forests
which strongly uphold environmental principles of Forest Stewardship.

scriptamanent

~

*To Sara, who gets me to see
the world differently through her beautiful eyes,
and to Charlotte, who constantly helps me to
discover things I had taken for granted.*

~

NAPOLEON THE COMMUNICATOR

8

NAPOLEON
THE VOICE OF A GENERATION

by Luigi Mascilli Migliorini
(European historian of the Napoleonic age)

No sooner had the twenty-seven-year-old general made his opening remarks than it became obvious that he was a natural born leader and communicator who comprised both the uncertainties of a Stendhalian hero and the arrogance of a Balzacian one. He had come to Nice in order to get acquainted with the high-ranking army officials who would fight at his side in the Italian Campaign. Nevertheless, he was viewed with mistrust by the elder men who suspected this shady general had been granted control of the army through political scheming and by portraying himself to be just like them; a product of The Revolution which allowed men with humble beginnings to rise to greatness. He was not the most experienced general at that time, however, he was able to win over his sceptics thanks to the clarity of his plans. In short, he convinced them that everyone should be the master of their own destiny rather than a passive observer at the service of The Revolution.

To put across the concept of The Revolution was nothing new. The Eighteenth Century had seen ideas swarm across European borders with consummate ease thanks to newspapers and weekly journals. It became a fad, setting people's minds on fire as to its possibilities. It could be considered a communication product, much like today's viral videos on the Internet. Obviously, this widespread propagation of ideas led to a multitude of conflicting and contrasting views. Despite all these conflicting messages, Napoleon managed to shape and convey his own original interpretation of this unique history-changing event. It scratched beneath the surface meaning as it contained hidden expectations and messages for the listener, which we would label as "subliminal" in today's language. Primarily, his first message is one of youth and rebirth, captured perfectly in 1796 when he addressed his soldiers by telling them about the march to "Europe's most fertile plains" at the start of the Italian Campaign. He convinced people that this was a new dawn of time, year zero. *"The slate of the past is to be wiped clean, history starts here"* was the message he wanted to convey. The Revolution reflects the hopes and expectations of each new generation. Naivety and ferocity stand cheek by jowl with shared suffering and dreams.

It is probably this iconic power of The Revolution, as conveyed by Napoleon, which is the main source of inspiration for the author to write this book. He feels challenged to harness Bonaparte's passion and intelligence from the more ambiguous aspect of his message. Starting from its initial noble call for equality and liberty among men, it transforms itself into a call to arms which requires all men to wear the same uniform within a single army whose quest is to establish the "Great" nation. This is most plainly seen on the day of the Battle of Austerlitz, when the cries of "Long live the Revolution" sounded by the soldiers in the Faubourg Saint Marcel, the fulcrum of Jacobean Paris, mingle with shouts of "Long live The Emperor", exclaimed by those loyal to The Old Guards. A cold imperial sun which mingles against the braziers of the egalitarian soldiers provides the backdrop to these opposing cries on the morning which will herald one of The Emperor's greatest victories.

Austerlitz is a watershed, being both the last Republican battle and the first Imperial one. This battle will mark a turning point, one which this book will endeavour to capture. The communal battle cry of the revolutionaries will now turn into the loneliness of the individual adventure. This is best illustrated just over one year later at Eylau, a battlefield which is a symbol of a savage loss of life, unlike Marengo and Arcole, which bathe the fighters in glory. At Eylau, we see Napoleon as a solitary figure, wrapped in his coat, the grave toll of victory evident on his face. The sad fact remains that all generations, even revolutionary ones, grow old. Those glowing heroic war reports of yesteryear from the times of the Italian and Egyptian Campaigns have been replaced with dreary uninspiring run-of-the-mill ones. This is best illustrated in the aftermath of the disastrous Russian Campaign in November 1812, which resulted in ignominious retreat and humiliating defeat on the River Beresina. Rather than give a true account of the events, the uninspiring dispatch reads thus: "The Emperor is in excellent health".

Obviously, the speed of communication back in Napoleonic times went at a snail's pace compared to the 21st century dizzying speed of the Internet. Back then, communiqués were far and few, and the author was forced to undergo thorough and time-consuming research. One significant fact which emerged was embedded within the communique issued at The Peace of Tilsit. Both Napoleon and Tsar Alexander met on a luxurious raft which bobbed idly on the River Nieman. Leisurely, they carved up the known world between them. Another significant communiqué pertained to the birth of Bonaparte's long-awaited heir. Despite the latter being given the title "King of Rome", he would not be spared a melancholy end. However, research was worth the effort and bore fruit. First of all, it provided a conclusive result. Secondly, it gives us an in-depth insight as to how Napoleon used certain mechanisms to build up and consolidate his power base in order to gain a swift and deep-rooted consensus. This research also sheds light on how the consensus is no longer just upheld by civil feats and military glory. Communication almost becomes pure narrative gesture.

❧

Napoleon's shooting star finally fell to earth. The Jacobites, who are weighed down by their extravagant uniforms and are more afraid of losing what they have won rather than pressing on and gaining the many prizes that are still at stake, decided to abandon the hero of their youth. It is the evening of 2nd August 1815 and aboard HMS Bellerofonte, Napoleon has just learnt that the British have decided to exile him to St Helena, a small island in the middle of the vast Atlantic Ocean. Ironically, as if fate had forewarned him, he had become aware of its remoteness while consulting an atlas as a young man. As can easily be imagined, bitter thoughts come back to haunt him. These were the same thoughts which had crossed his mind only a few months earlier immediately after his defeat at Waterloo. His loss of faith and trust, the betrayal of his friends; all of this made the defeated man's solitude even bitterer and left him without hope. *"My dear friend"* he says to his listener *""I have the desire to abandon you, and I would not find it difficult to do so. All it would take is a rush of blood to the head and I would be off like a shot"*.

Those who heard these words were cut to the quick. *"A man of his stature could not drag himself down to such a lowly level as if he were a broken gambler or a betrayed lover. It is the reply of someone who, having abandoned the idea of taking his own life, is now wondering how he might fill his days in this god-forsaken place in the middle of nowhere and reacts by saying "We shall write our memoirs".* This is how Napoleon's final battle, one of communication, unfolded as the defeated and forlorn Emperor exchanged a few remarks with his travelling companion, Count Emanuel de Las Cases. It would prove to be his most spectacular and significant, overshadowing all the real battle victories that he had achieved in his days of glory. To tell tales and narrate one's life with clarity, as the boat makes it way towards the open sea, takes on the significance of life having the upper hand over death. The words which came into being through action survive the latter. They are the words of someone who is taking leave of the present, no longer interested in winning a consensus from fickle contemporaries and bequeathing everything to future generations. *"The Saint Helena Memoir"* will become one of the nineteenth century's best-sellers. It will serve as a Bible for two generations of young men filled with both ambition and disenchantment, who just like Julien Sorel, the hero of Stendhal's "Le Rouge et le Noir" consider all books to be mendacious and written by morally bankrupt writers in order to gain promotion. By disregarding his peers, who have grown old and have made progress through crafty manoeuvring and a lust for money, Napoleon is able to address a new budding generation which is still uncontaminated by an inconclusive Revolution and by an Empire which never really took off. His narrative voice is not that of a world weary 50 year-old but rather that of his 20 year-old self, a youthful dreamer who believed that anything was possible.

Just how many Internet sites are dedicated to Napoleon Bonaparte? Furthermore, how many social networks, be they Instagram, Facebook or Twitter, or even Hashtags, are connected to this great historical figure? Over the last years, just how many meetings, special events and debates have been dedicated to The Emperor? Is it possible to enumerate the number of clubs, associations and groups which try to keep his memory alive? How many books have been written about him? How many works of art, objects, tin soldiers, cartoon figures spring directly from his likeness? Just how many films have paid homage to him? Rather than showing any signs of fading, this phenomenon seems to be snowballing. It is a self-perpetuating phenomenon. The best example of this in Italy is the extraordinary prize winning novel "N" written by Ernesto Ferrara, which was then made into a blockbuster film by Paolo Virzì. There are constant re-enactments of his most famous battles from Austerlitz to Waterloo, played out all over the world by aficionados. Myth is transformed into reality. He has even influenced fashion and interior decoration.

Today, a Napoleonic market exists, and it generates a turnover that easily exceeds seven figures. Leaving aside the self-fulfilling prophecies he made on the remote Atlantic island of Saint Helena, it cannot be denied that his work has left a mark on time that has turned to be much greater than his enemies, the self-declared winners, could ever have imagined. Their victory turned out to be a pyrrhic one. This is not only due to the fact that his liberal ideas, his administrative and legislative reforms, and his setting up of new bourgeois cultural models ensured that there would be no backward return to the past, but also because the man himself exists outside the rigid constraints of time.

Napoleon is not a Homeric hero in the strict sense of the word. He could be considered an archetype of this, despite being a modern-age player. He has a certain magical quality which makes him timeless and sets him apart from the other great men of his era and successive ones. The twentieth century and its two great wars have not produced a similar character. Of course, there is the phenomenon of Adolph Hitler, but in this case, it is the embodiment of absolute evil which both horrifies and fascinates the onlooker. It is difficult to conceive how much intellectual and physical hatred is able to hold the masses in its thrall. Napoleon is something completely different. Despite being a dictator, he could never be conceived as a tyrant. He is a complex figure riddled with contradictions, the heir of revolutionary ideas which filled him with compassion for others, despite his thirst for absolute power.

This does not explain, however, his long lasting popularity nearly 200 years after his death. He was a great general and a brilliant military tactician who won countless battles. But so too were Julius Caesar, Giuseppe Garibaldi, and Dwight Eisenhower, the D-Day hero who had his famous success 150 years after the Emperor's demise. Despite the latter's historic success, he was never able to achieve anything near what the miraculous Napoleon did. Simply put, he was born, lived and died a winner, unlike all the aforementioned.

Furthermore, Napoleon was also a great statesman as well as being a promoter of codification and an art lover. This complex character stuck to the concept of totalitarian rule which was prevalent at the time, whilst at the same time, he managed to bring into being a number of historical processes and yet be ahead of the times. This turned out to be his winning card, thus allowing him to become a modern legend reaching out from beyond the grave. Simply put, he was a great communicator at all levels. He was the first statesman who saw beyond short-term consensus as he was aware that it had to span the coming centuries and extend to successive generations. Unlike previous rulers, he did not limit himself to superficially pleasing the bourgeoisie and the masses. He mulled over all possible implications, fully aware that his grip on power depended on gaining the support of all the social classes by creating something tangible and concrete for everyone. Communication for Napoleon meant being one step ahead of your enemy and then routing him. For him, setting up a summit is just the same as commissioning a work of art. Whether it be a success on the battlefield or the creation of legislation both within and outside France, everything must be conceived as a victory by his followers.

Napoleon got his message across by being at the forefront of fashion, ideas, stylishness and trends. He could be considered a pioneer in merchandising, as well as being the brains behind systems of wartime interaction, not dissimilar to how leading companies operate now. Furthermore, he was the founder, censor and comptroller of the press. His popularist war-bulletins could be considered the prototype for today's advertising leaflets or fliers. Finally, his N and the eagle on the imperial standard mark him out as the inventor of modern logos and brands.

Many Napoleonic institutions made their mark in various contexts throughout the twentieth century and even into the first decade of the new millennium. The common denominator springs from his great communicative skill which ensures that everything has a communicative message and portrays a man who both perpetuates an idea and creates something new and radical.

Napoleon, moreover, was victorious as the grand communicator, due to the fact that the fairy tale he was telling was far from being an ordinary one. It is the extraordinary undertaking of a man who was able to combine a revolutionary spirit with a conservative one. This inimitable military strategist was also an enlightened innovator who combined equal amounts of ambition and pragmatism. The codification of the law, the modernization of public administration, the setting up of the great national schools and the dismantling of the feudal system all bear witness to this.

※

Napoleon's contributions played a major role in writing European and French history in the years to follow, thus paving the way for the creation of numerous institutions. In one of fate's strange twists, in 2016 I started working at one of the largest Italian financial institutions, Borsa Italiana - London Stock Exchange Group, which is the result of Napoleon's initial steps taken to set up the pillars for what would later become the first Exchange in Milan. Indeed, it was the Viceroy Eugenio Napoleon who penned the document sanctioning the setting up of a stock exchange in Milan, then capital of the Italian Kingdom, on the 16th of January, 1808. The document decreed the establishement of an "Exchange of Commerce in Milan in virtue of the authority delegated by the highest emperor and King Napoleon 1".

1
BUILDING UP THE IMAGE

How a guttersnipe manages to grab and sustain power
by putting himself across as the champion for a new society
based on universal rights and opportunities

1.1 Between the soldiers and the Directory

"Soldiers, you stand naked and are badly fed. The government owes you so much
yet can give you nothing. The patience and courage you display on this barren
ground is admirable, yet it brings you no glory. No light is shed on you. I wish
to lead you to more fertile plains. Rich provinces and great cities will be at your
mercy. You shall find honour, glory and wealth".

With this opening proclamation of the 1796 Italian Campaign, Napoleon addresses an army which is far removed from the outcast rag-tag masses of the
past. These were soldiers who had fought under the command of a noble lord
simply to be able to procure food and avoid starvation. Being a soldier was the
lesser of evils compared to the day-to-day subsistence and squalor of the country or the slums of the big towns. Napoleon's citizen soldiers are a new breed,
even if they descend from the same anthropological background. What has definitively changed them is not just the overthrowing of the old order by means
of The Revolution, but also their general's skill in motivating them.

Napoleon has changed the rules of the game. A soldier is no longer just someone who carries out orders but someone who contributes to the betterment
of society. He enables constant room for improvement. Stalling is a crime. No
longer will the 'status quo' be allowed to remain untouched. Defensive tactics,
which were the norm before the Italian Campaign, have been abandoned. The
betterment of society is based on winning new territory and wealth. Napoleon's
lucid determination not only manages to spur on his troops, but also to overturn the previously sceptical attitude of the commanders of the armed forces,

who were far from enamoured with the legitimacy of The Directory's decision. As Luigi Mascilli Migliorini points out in his book "Napoleon", all Bonaparte had to do was: *"make them understand that he was no petty official protected by Barras, but rather that he was on the same wavelength as them, wanting to shake up society in the aftermath of The Revolution in order to win their trust"*.

The crop of victories resulting from the Italian Campaign which established him as a great military leader, pushed him to portray himself as a thorn in The Directory's side. Napoleon's effrontery is evident the day after conquering Lombardy, when he replies to the notification of the peace treaty signed between France and Sardinia. It would have been enough to say that he had read it, yet he says "The Army approves of it".

Similar shows of effrontery quickly resulted in hostility towards Bonaparte within the government who was quite aware that his popularity with and influence on his soldiers could result in him taking absolute power. With this in mind, the government attempted to place General Francois Kellermann alongside him in the Italian Campaign in order to quell their anxiety. The ignominious reversal of this decision by The Directory illustrates just how weak they were in respect to this military leader who, if he had so wished, could have turned the army against those supposedly in power.

It was enough for Napoleon to say, more ironically than with contempt or anger: *"One bad general is better than two good ones put together"* to ensure the government reconsidered their original proposal regarding Kellermann. The risks did not lie in what was actually said, rather they were inherent within the threats and hidden dangers.

In the meantime, Napoleon could afford to adopt strong words and derisory behaviour, as he was confident of the support of public opinion. He had been able to win over this public support, not only as a result of his military victories, but also because of the way he shared the glory with his soldiers and the general public. The most important segment of the general public was the middle class upon whom he founded and legitimized his new power base acquired through ten years of civil war. The Italian Campaign was not quite over, yet Napoleon had become the brightest star in the firmament.

As Emil Ludwig states in his 'Napoleon', *"Paris is happy to have a new hero after years of waiting. His face dominates all the shop windows, he is eulogised in poetry, and the most famous actors constantly mention him. His trophies are on show in the Luxembourg courtyard. His dispatches, censored by The Directory, appear in 'Le Moniteur'. Songs are written about him, coins bearing his image are minted. Even caricatures arrive from England. All these things delight the boulevards. The only ones who are not laughing are the members of The Directory".*

The man founds his power-base upon the army. He is a formidable beast which cannot be taken lightly. At the same time, the young general skilfully handles his relations with the government. He is always able to obtain the sending of further reinforcements by threatening a disaster, the repercussions of which will reach the seat of power itself. *"Maybe the hour will come for the valorous Charles Augereau; the intrepid André Massena, Louis Berthier and even for myself . What will then befall our trusty soldiers? This thought holds me back. I no longer dare challenge death, it would only dishearten and dismay those in our charge".* As a swift counterpoint to this thinly veiled threat, mentioned by Ludwig in his biography of The Emperor, Napoleon makes amends by rewarding the government handsomely with booty captured in his Italian Campaign. An example of this is the gift he sends from Milan, accompanied with his statement: *"To a threadbare government surrounded by heaps of worthless banknotes, I send you a hundred of the best horses I have managed to find in Lombardy. Let them replace the tired nags which are currently pulling your carriages"* Napoleon was definitely a master at using the "stick and the carrot" approach.

◆

The Corsican does not hide his privileged relationship with the seat of power from his men. He is fully aware that cohesion between a leader and his troops can transcend the boundaries of the battle field in as far as it is a united effort which wins the day. Hence, the spoils should not just be left to him and his closest collaborators. Together and as one, they are a power whose strength and successes fully deserve to be rewarded. Napoleon, therefore, does his utmost to make his men realise just how important military victories are for the "health" of the newly created French state. In the Proclamation of Mantua, for example, he underlines this by saying: *"The revenue levied from the conquered countries have fed, clothed and provided wages for the army during the campaign. Furthermore, you have sent thirty million to the Ministry of Finance, to replenish the public coffers. You have also enriched the Museum of Paris with over three hundred masterpieces from both ancient and modern Italy. Works of art whose production took thirty centuries".*

1.2 The Democracy of Arms

The relationship between Napoleon and his soldiers did not consist of duplicity or double dealing. This would remain constant, even in the period of The Empire, in keeping with meritocracy and democracy. As Stendhal noted: *"On the front, after a victory, or even just a breakthrough by a certain division, the Emperor would, without fail, review his troops. After having stopped amongst the ranks, accompanied by the colonel, and having spoken with all the soldiers present, he would have a military ban prepared. The officials stood around him and if a squadron leader had been killed in action, he would ask aloud "Who is the most valiant captain among you?" There, in the heat of the moment after a victory, the responses were sincere and spontaneous. Should it transpire that the most valiant captain did not possess the necessary qualifications, Napoleon ensured that this soldier was promoted within 'le Legion d'Honneur', after which he tackled the issue afresh by asking "After him, who is the next most valiant?"*.

His soldiers' faith in him bordered on veneration sprung from a frank and open relationship. Nevertheless, this did not spare them the rod nor criticism when The Emperor deemed it necessary. Those who stepped out of line or endangered others would inevitably feel the full force of his wrath. From the very first battle, Napoleon made it patently clear where everyone stood. This is how, for example, he settled a score, in one of his dispatches dated 7 November 1796. He publicly humiliates those under his command who he considered not to be up to the task by saying: *"Soldiers, I am not at all happy with you. You have neither shown discipline nor steadfastness nor bravery by not standing your ground. You fled in blind terror, your cowardice yielded a position from which a handful of valiant troops could have held off an entire army. Soldiers of the 39th and 85th regiments, you are not French soldiers! General, Chief of Staff, have it written on the flags, they no longer belong to our Italian Division"*.

Besides, there is no one else who knows the art of motivation better than Napoleon. As Alex Suchet highlights in his French language book 'Napoleon et le management', achieving emulation and to lead by example comes more easily in extreme situations, and in the military field Napoleon is incomparable. In his opinion *"courage cannot be faked, it is a virtue which is not contaminated by hypocrisy. Throughout the course of his military career, Napoleon has displayed the same physical courage he demands from his men. Despite being fully aware of the attendant danger, he always displayed an amazing cool in the heat of the battle"*. Napoleon embodies both the supreme judge and the great motivator, yet he delivers new strategies based on conquests achieved on the battle field rather than those based on birth and class. He is an irreplaceable guide and comes across as the most valiant of all.

His superiority is not just simply a result of bravery. *"Had they not known that I was the most educated, then all would have been lost"*. He is entitled to command thanks to superior intelligence and schooling. This, however, does not prove to be negative, nor does it drive a wedge between him and his men. There is a bond between Napoleon and his men which did not previously exist between the subjects and the king at the time of the Ancién Regime. During inspections of the Grande Armée, The Emperor would wear the standard grey and lilac uniform. It was his way of saying *"I am one of you"*, but it also conveyed the following message: *"I am the only one who can understand you, so I am the only one who can lead you"*. This image, inevitably, has to be backed up by facts. The two million francs of gold given out along with the other benefits which were granted after the victory at Austerlitz bear witness to just how efficient the Emperor's strategy was. However, he did not simply buy the affection of his troops with filthy lucre. Their bond was much stronger than money. He wasn't simply just paying mercenaries. Paradoxically with Napoleon, fundamental requisites of the Revolution are consolidated when its foundations are uprooted both in the dramatic sense as well as in the atavistic struggle for existence. He embodies the real life affirmation of social conquests which were overshadowed in the turmoil of the Revolution itself. Rewards and money are fundamental, yet, belief in your fellow man, and admiration or even veneration for someone who has positively transformed your life by guiding you step by step are just as important.

❧

In this context, the language of words and gestures is part of the magic. The triumph of Austerlitz came about on 2 December 1805. Only three days earlier, Napoleon had received a Russian ambassador who had bought him the terms and conditions regarding a truce. The ambassador's approach was somewhat arrogant. The French army had yielded ground on their position as if they feared facing the enemy. Napoleon did not react to the ambassador's contempt to defend national pride or to upbraid him for his lack of respect in addressing the French Emperor. He merely remained passive, taking in the ambassador's words, looking meek and concerned, giving the impression that he fully understood the precarious situation his army was in, both from a military and tactical point of view. This stance was also part of his communications' arsenal. A reverse poker bluff. No sooner had he dismissed the ambassador than he explained to his men that he saw a certain victory looming with each minute that passed. *"That man is blinded by his arrogance. He thinks we fear them. He is playing into our hands"*.

Indeed, Austerlitz was like a delicately-tuned trap which snapped shut just when Napoleon had timed it to do so. It consisted of a finely woven mesh of manoeuvres and ruses. It could be considered as Bonaparte's master stroke, however he would always give the deserved credit to his high ranking officers and the entire army as a whole. On the eve of the battle, on 30 December, Bonaparte addressed his troops with a speech which played on the deepest of passions and emotions without ever once sinking into empty rhetoric. Perhaps in his most effective dispatch ever, he is reported to have said: *"Should the outcome of the battle ever be in doubt, you will see your Emperor himself fight on the front line, because victory cannot be compromised when the honour of the French infantry is at stake"*. Once again, the message is crystal clear: *"I am one of you"*. A defeat is unimaginable, because it will not be Napoleon who loses, but rather the glorious French infantry. It is the speech of a general who wishes to be a leader but not a tyrant. He wants everybody to understand and to fully contribute to what is about to happen. The glue which holds everything together and eventually wins the day is the awareness of and the faith in the rightness of the planned strategy. Only if everyone plays their part, will everything go as planned and the enemy will be defeated. Napoleon is also able to be reassuring and deliver on his promises. *"A victory will bring our campaign to an end and we will be able to retreat to our winter quarters where we will meet up with other divisions which have been formed in France"*. War is followed by peace. After all the effort and danger, the soldiers will have their well-earned rest and will be able to wind down in the company of their fellow soldiers.

Napoleonic vocabulary constantly mentions joint aims, intent, values and shared experiences. The most common possessive adjective used is the first person plural, such as: *"our campaign"* or *"our quarters"*. Not only does he make his troops feel included, his communication masterpieces also provide them with reassuring details of what will happen. He is sharing his plans, hopes and ambitions with them. He is showing them that victory is already in the bag. He is giving out assurances, whereby he states: *"our position is impregnable. As the enemy advance to attack us on the right, they will expose their flank"*. The soldiers can rest assured that their general is ahead of the enemy and that their endeavours will be facilitated by the leader's tactical genius. He lets them know that the enemy is about to walk into the trap as they did at Ulm (which Napoleon purposely mentions in his speech). Once inside, they are doomed.

When words were not enough, it was time for deeds. On the evening subsequent to his address, he undertook a ten-kilometre horse ride in order to inspect all his troops. This was something which had never been seen nor had it happened previously. Napoleon wanted to underline his supremacy by making himself seen. It seems to be his way of saying, *"You have always won for me, you will win once again"*. Both young and old got the message, as the air was filled with cries of "Vive l'Empereur". This feeling of respect was not lost on Napoleon and he did his utmost to maintain it. One way of doing this was by exchanging compliments. After Austerlitz, not only was he generous with his financial rewards but he was just as generous in expressing his gratitude. Who else could have known just how important the victory had been both in the historical and symbolic sense? Writing in his 'Napoleon', Alexandre Dumas states that victory at Austerlitz: *"... was for the Empire what the victory at Marengo had been for the Consulate. It sanctioned the past and heralded the power of the future"*. Slowly but surely, he placed his men in positions of power in the various states and statelets which had fallen within the orbit of the mighty France, examples of these being the Kingdom of the two Sicilies, The Batavian Republic, The Kingdom of Holland and The Grand Duchy of Berg. *"Napoleon does not hold a sceptre in his hand"* emphasises the author of The Three Musketeers and The Count of Monte Cristo *"but rather a globe"*. Addressing his troops, he informs them that they have routed an army which was numerically superior. He will fire up their pride prior to their return to France to celebrate by saying: "All you will have to say is *"I fought at Austerlitz"* and people will reply you are a truly valiant man".

This comradely bond with his troops will stand fast, even during the later dark moments such as his removal from the throne after the invasion of Paris and his exile to Elba. His taking up arms once again, his return to France, and the retrieval of his leadership role were all facilitated by the fact that he continued to enjoy huge popularity, not only amongst the civilian population, but also amongst the royalist army which, ironically, had been put in place to prevent him from doing so. The most emblematic episode which took place near Grenoble is recorded by Stendhal, *"Napoleon brought his grenadiers to a halt and, unaccompanied, made his way to the battalion. As he drew close to them, he halt-ed abruptly and opened his coat.* "It is I" *he exclaimed,* "Please show your recogni-tion. Should there be anyone amongst you who would like to kill the Emperor, he is invited to draw fire now, the time has come". Simply by making this dramatic gesture, he won them all over. The air was filled with cries of "Long live The Emperor" as the soldiers threw themselves into each other's arms.

1.3 Interacting with Others

Just who were the common people for Napoleon? Maybe it would be better to take a closer look at the importance he began to assign to the middle classes immediately after his first gains in the Italian campaign. This was the class that ascended in terms of power and economic clout. Despite the power they had gained, they were still filled with anxiety vis-à-vis the ongoing political and so-cial instability which resulted from the taking of The Bastille. This was further accentuated after the terrible events of 1793 immediately after the Revolution. The middle class was desperate for a strong leader, one capable of bringing about a quelling of social tensions and a process of social rebalancing. This required members of the middle class to sacrifice some of their hard earned freedoms, without yielding other various power gains extracted from the third estate. Nevertheless, their desire and desperation were strong enough to gener-ate interest in any signal which might mark a turnaround in trends regarding the breaking up and weakness of the political landscape.

To this end, the cascade of military victories accomplished by a rising young star from the army, who was able to transform a defensive campaign into a victory for post-revolutionary France, turned out to be well-timed and conven-ient. News of these victories spread like wild fire and it was not long before the road in which the new general lived was renamed *Rue de la Victoire*.

From the very beginning of the campaign, Napoleon skilfully exploited his dispatches to inform people back home about the successes and aims of what would come to be known as la Grande Armée. By paying a great deal of at-tention to the form and content of his communications, the young general endeavoured to put across the ideals of the Revolution, making his mark on foreign territories as a liberator rather than an oppressor. Although inwardly he has become disenchanted with many of its ideals, as a cunning and ambitious protagonist of a new historical era, he milks the Revolution for what he can by holding it up as a vehicle of hope for a new society of free men. This is the message he conveys to the Italians at the end of his Proclamation delivered on

26 April 1796. *"People of Italy"*, he thunders in his typical pragmatic rhetoric, *"The French army has come to break your chains. We French are everybody's friends. Do not fear us. Your property, religion and costumes will all be respected. In war we are generous enemies as the only thing we despise are the tyrants who hold you in bondage".* This speech was a master piece in astuteness. He wanted to form a consensus beyond the boundaries of France. He was preparing victory by smoothing out the way ahead for an occupying power which will govern rather than repress. He was well aware that French dominance could grow and develop by playing on the emotional concepts of nationhood and freedom, which the Revolution had stirred up in other countries then subsequently exploited to its own advantage.

⬧

Members of the educated middle-class and many intellectuals who had initially allowed themselves to be taken in by the words of the Great Communicator, were bitterly disappointed. Sometime later, Ugo Foscolo expresses the abrupt awakening of many Italians to the reality of life after Campoformio, in one of his famous letters to Jacopo Ortis. *"Our country's sacrifice is in tatters. Everything is lost. Even though our lives will be spared, there is nothing we can do but weep for our misfortune and woe. I know my name to be on the blacklist, but do you expect me to hand myself over to those who betrayed me in order to save myself from those who oppress me?"*
NNevertheless, in Italy, just as in Egypt, Napoleon sacrifices all requests or petitions to his own personal design, to which he links a re-composition based on post-revolutionary France. His self-portrayal constantly remains at the forefront, whereby he tries, whenever possible, to utilize this image of himself to achieve military triumphs and civilian advances, some of which were real, while others were imaginary. Without a shadow of a doubt, it was the great leader himself who was the driving force behind these propagations of the deeds and feats of the Italian Campaign Army. In the summer of 1797, our hero founds the two publications *'Le Courrier de l'Armée d'Italie'* and *'La France vue de l'Armée d'Italie'* in order to gain access to the mass of readers, whose political and economic clout had substantially increased. Hence, by acting as a *'vox-pops'* and by attempting to gauge their moods and aspirations, in addition to catering to their whims, he effectively weakens and annihilates the Sun King's grip on power.
Having attained the position of First Consul, Bonaparte decided to relocate to *Les Tuileries.* This was a highly symbolic act to show that the new leaders of

France were now ensconced in the old Bourbon residence. He will go on to say, however, to his secretary Louis Antoine Fauvelet de Bourienne: *"moving into Les Tuileries is not everything, it is staying there which is important"*. How will he succeed in doing this? By ambivalent behaviour and actions which will mark his dictatorship. Napoleon broke away from the people with the very same instruments which he had used to win over their trust. On Christmas Day 1799, he officially declares the Revolution defunct, declaring that the reasons that had brought it about were riddled with shortcomings which contradicted the principles of a popular upheaval.

The people had been released from the Revolution's restrictive cage, but from now on, as one former revolutionary will comment, *"They will act for him in its name, but no longer will it be done in the manner of a madcap spontaneous stampede"*. Of the three consuls, it was Bonaparte alone who had clear ideas as to how this process might be carried out. He knows that the people have grown weary of unstable government. He is also aware that freedom is nothing more than a mere word rather than an integral part of popular culture. He maintains that: *"The Republic is nothing more than a passing fad which has turned the people's heads and which will gradually wane like all previous fads. What they really want is glory and to have their vanity sated. They know absolutely nothing about freedom"*. At the beginning, however, this stance does not prevent him from paying lip service to the previous regime. For the French people, he remains "Citizen Consul". A very special citizen to whom they entrust their need for peace. Bonaparte also doesn't consider turning back the hands of time. It is a question of rebuilding a new French society whose only lasting mark risks being the physical and spiritual debris brought about at the end of the Eighteenth Century. Bonaparte's most significant contribution to the rebuilding of France is the Napoleonic Code, the setting up of a modern administration. This is jointly agreed upon with The Church, thus bringing an end to the anti-clerical campaign and the attendant hatred which grew in the years of the so-called "Terror". Its repercussions would also be felt throughout Europe as it brought about modernization. As Napoleon sets out his stall, he does not forget to "speak" to others.

Special importance is given to The Louvre, the trove of universal culture where works of art are stored, all of them being the result of pillage during the Italian and Egyptian campaigns. Furthermore, much space was dedicated to the Great Leader within the confines of the very same building. Napoleon was on a roll, conducting a marketing campaign both at home and abroad. The aim of this campaign was to link up the new power base in France with a new higher vision of historical and social values, with him, The Great Leader, at the centre of it. Napoleon also made use of court pomp and ceremonies to develop his ambivalent Napoleonic Code. Since the monarchy had been defeated, the protector of the people had become a de-facto king in as far as the trappings of luxury, such as sumptuous clothing and jewellery ordained and embellished his power. This time, however, the people were happy with this situation. There is a constant interchange between keeping his distance from the masses and "being one of the boys". He initiated the prototype walkabout, so popular with today's politicians. He would willingly engage in a quick exchange of views with an elderly lady one day, then the next he would become unreachable covered in the sweeping pomp of a great parade. He had The Tuileries lined with statues of Alexander the Great and Julius Caesar, in addition to those of Scipio, Marcus Brutus, George Washington and Honoré Gabriel Riqueti Count of Mirabeau.

For Napoleon, style could never be equal to substance. It was deeds which shaped every single person's destiny, including his own. His pragmatism did not stop him, however, from spotting, with incredible institution and innovation, the levers which could enhance and increase his successes, both as a soldier and as a statesman. His amazing eye for detail effectively resulted in his creation of the concept of merchandising in the true sense of the word.

Imperial style is the ordainment of the originality of his figure. The child and heir of The Revolution renews the pomp and splendour of the past, inspiring a wide-ranging artistic movement examples of which are the works of architects such as *Charles Percier* and *Pierre-François-Léonard Fontaine*.

⁂

The man exudes an extraordinary charm which even influenced women's fashion and tastes. At the beginning of the nineteenth century, his influence radically changed women's clothing and bearing. Garments were worn with ordered severity and the favoured hairstyle was the classically-groomed flowing locks. Furniture was now made in mahogany and rosewood. The sumptuousness and consistency of the brocades and embroidery served to flaunt the rebirth of imperial times. Napoleon, in this sense, foreshadowed the Mussolini era by drawing inspiration from Caesar and imperial Rome. The famous Napoleonic N and the symbolic choice of the eagle, both of which were not there by accident, helped to materially, spiritually, and morally mark an extraordinary era. Once again, the Emperor was ahead of the times.

The N logo is as essential as it is ingenious. It becomes ubiquitous over the three decades of Napoleonic dominance. It can be found everywhere. It is embossed in books and pictures and engraved on large and small objects alike. It is even to be found on sculptures. In short, it might be considered the prototype brand and the forerunner to modern design. The increasing endorsement of the legend is proportionate to the French people's enthusiasm to turn him into a living deity. A number of grotesque and amusing titles, such as that of Saint Napoleon, arose from the gap created by the anti-religious fervour born from the Revolution, and the Emperor's crafty rehabilitation, as he was only too aware of the link between temporal and religious power. This was done to fill in the void, however, it prevented the great Corsican from celebrating his name day. Using the eagle as an icon, or what would be called a "brand" in today's modern terminology, for the Grande Armée, was not a casual decision. Quite the contrary, it was the fruit of thousands of hours of study, after a commission was set up for this particular purpose.

Napoleon foreshadows the theories of modern marketing when it comes to target segments. To use the language of modern marketing guru Philip Kotler, he knew who he wanted to get the message across to, who he was competing with, and the pitch upon which the battle would be fought.
The consistency with which he referred to the imperial eagle, whether in speeches, iconography, or on other specific occasions clearly shows how lucidly aware he was of what we would call informed brand policy in today's language. The following three examples best sum this up. A few days after his coronation on 5 December 1804, he attends the ceremony in which the eagles are handed out at the Champ de Mar *"Here are your standards"* he tells his soldiers. *"These eagles will serve as a moral bond and will hold you together. Your Emperor will place them wherever he deems it necessary for the defence of his throne and his people"*. In the dispatch issued at Strasbourg on 30 September of the following year before the Austrian campaign he states: *"Endeavour to overcome any obstacle and do not rest until the eagle has been planted in enemy soil"*. The final example regards the anti-Russian proclamation drawn up in December at the imperial quarters in Posen 1806 which declared: *"In vain, the Russians have sought to seize the capital of this ancient and illustrious Poland, yet now it is the French eagle which is proudly waving on the banks of the Vistola"*.
Yet this symbolism is also necessary for Napoleon to be able to consolidate public opinion and sway the people into placing their trust in the absolute superiority of the most dominant figure of the time. The wildfire growth and

distribution of objects depicting our Corsican hero underpins a people's enthusiasm for a guttersnipe who grabbed power from those who had held on to it for centuries based solely on "Divine Will". Despite his great achievements so far, the Emperor cannot afford to rest on his laurels. His godlike status is the fruit of social and political recognition. His dictatorship will only remain intact if accompanied by popular consensus. The marketing connected to Napoleon's image, which endorses and enhances the cult of personality, strengthens the legitimacy of the Emperor.

1.4 Paintings

The triumphant depiction of Napoleon as he crosses The Saint Bernard Pass has, over the course of the centuries, become an emblem of the second victorious Italian campaign. It was commissioned by Napoleon himself to the artist Jacques Louis David. It pays full tribute to his historical role and the implications of his deeds from 18 Brumaire onwards. Bonaparte gives precise instructions to the artist, telling him to portray him as calm while atop a fiery steed. The resulting image is unreal, showing the head of the French army riding on a dirt track on which it would have been impossible to mount the saddle of a thoroughbred horse. Yet, despite the exaggerated plasticity of the horse, and its exasperated air which seems to make it look more like a toy than a real animal, the end result conveys seriousness and composure. The dominant central figure, of course is Napoleon, and it is his presence which resolves any contradictions. His face radiates awareness of his historical function. His features are classical and sober, even in triumph. Napoleon is still young and has a long and hard road ahead of him. He is well aware of this, and this is what makes him great. He will show which way to go. In his cool control over immediate events, his conviction of having to look ahead is clearly written. He will lead his men *"over the pass"*. The creation of his legend in this painting is a leitmotif of how the future Emperor will henceforth continue with his lucid strategies.

The legend is indeed an ennoblement of a falsehood. There were many in the second Italian campaign which were then given a positive spin by the winner. Reality was much more gruesome and complex. A fine example of this is the reality gap between what happened at the battle of Marengo and the winners' account of it. Such incongruities had already been noted by certain witnesses at the time, such as the writer and diplomat François-René de Chateaubriand.

In his posthumous book *Memories from beyond the Grave* he points out the anomalies in David's picture regarding weather conditions. Napoleon "*crosses the San Bernard pass on a fiery steed in the middle of a blizzard when, in reality, the weather was fine!*".

◆

An episode linked to the previous happy experience, the successes of the first Italian campaign, helps to shift the attention of the great leader towards the communicative potential of iconography. While attempting to cross the bridge at Arcole, near Verona in 1797, the Corsican allegedly grabbed a flag and charged straight towards the Austrian artillery. This incident had an unhappy and inglorious conclusion, as both horse and rider plummeted into the River Alpone below. His subsequent triumphs had so fired up enthusiasm among the general public, that the artist Antoine-Jean Gros was commissioned to actually immortalize him. Napoleon agreed to pose for the painter in Milan and introduced his first wife Josephine to him. The outcome of this session was an overturning of historical fact. What had actually been a mishap at Arcole, is portrayed on canvas as a turning point which led to victory in the Italian campaign. The young unkempt general is portrayed in a combination of cool-headedness and boldness, brandishing the French standard and leading his soldiers to victory.

In this pictorial representation, Napoleon is no longer on his horse but on foot. Rather than immortalizing him as a general, the painter Antoine-Jean Gros is more concerned in portraying him as the leading light of the Revolution, with the colours of the French flag wrapped around his neck. With his long flowing unkempt hair, Napoleon is the polar opposite of how he is usually portrayed, whereby maturity and even old age are the attributes which denote power and military conquest. The fable of Arcole lies in the exaltation and distortion of this particular action, which sets Napolean apart despite all the other heroic deeds of his companions. An example of these heroic deeds is when general Augereau went forward brandishing the tricolour in the face of enemy fire before Bonaparte did. A salvo of shots which, when the Corsican tried to advance, had already mortally wounded his aide-de-champ, Jean-Baptiste Muiron, who had used his body to shield the young future Emperor. The battle took place between 15 and 17 November 1796 and it was not on that first day, as is recorded by the majority of history books, that it was won by the French. Yet, despite everything, the man of Arcole had a sweeping success. Gros' painting, which is of outstanding beauty, went on to inspire many replicas. Not just more paintings, but also carvings and even a monument many years later in 1808. This goes to show just how aware Bonaparte was, even as a young man, of the need to promote his image beyond the battlefield.

It could be said that he scored a bullseye in doing this, achieving more than he could ever have done in his wildest dreams. Not even he could have imagined that one of the first ever films, an artistic medium yet to be invented at his time, would be dedicated to him and his exploits. It was produced by Alice Guy in 1898 for the Gaumont film company and bore the title: *"Bonaparte au pont d'Arcole"*. It was the Italian campaign which would serve as a major source for strengthening the myth of the Corsican on the big screen. The most famous example of this is Abel Gance's Napoleon produced in 1927.

In 1804, Gros made a new contribution with another graphic paean to the iconography of Napoleon when portraying an episode from the Syrian expedition. The general's posterity is captured on canvas, showing him as he runs his finger along a plague victim's sore in Jaffa. The Corsican general is portrayed as a great humanitarian. Compassion and pain is written all over his face. The message which the observer receives is that the cast-iron solidarity between the general and his soldiers on the battle field, does not diminish in times of trouble, even if it means risking his own health. What the picture does not tell us is that Napoleon, despite his magnanimity displayed on canvas, decided to have all plague victims poisoned so as not to hamper operations and remove all burdens. This picture was to earn Gros, who studied at the David school, the title of official painter. He had already been in the general's court entourage for a good many years, having even been in the artistic commission whose task it was to decide which paintings were to be pillaged on foreign expeditions and brought back to France.

Perhaps the most notable of all this Parisian painter's works which uses the artistic function as a means of promoting the myth of the superman who led the French, is the one of Napoleon on the battlefield at Eylau (1807). This goes beyond mere exaltation. Something has changed after Jena. For the moment, the mood is not tangible, but it would seem the French people's faith in the Corsican general's redeeming qualities is slowly starting to wane, despite his continued successes. It would seem that the price paid in blood and casualties on the part of the soldiers and indirectly by the civilian population is much too high.

Given the general slaughter, public opinion is now in favour of peace in order to avoid further pointless sacrifices. With half of Europe fighting against him in various coalitions which had been re-energised after the various defeats, Napoleon was beginning to lose the faith and trust of those who had believed in him. The battle of Eylau is the most relevant example of how the cruel contradiction of fate was about to shape the Emperor's destiny over the next decade or so. The Grande Armée emerges victorious once again, but at what price! In his "Memoires", Jean-Baptiste Marbot will write: *"There was a terrible slaughter; in a fit of fury, the cuirassiers, appalled at the losses of their hussar and dragoon comrades, wiped out the eight Russian battalions! The enemy was either slaughtered or taken prisoner. The battlefield was truly a scene of horror"*. 'Gros' painting was declared the winner in a competition set up by the director of the Louvre, Vivant Denon, immediately after news from the battlefield of Eylau which spoke not only of the victory, but also of tragedy. The purpose was to reinvigorate public morale and reawaken French pride at a time when the situation threatened to spiral out of control. This time, the official painter Gros, while celebrating yet another Napoleonic triumph in his work, does not neglect to portray the horror and the price that this victory cost in human terms. The ground is strewn with corpses which, for the most part, are all wearing Russian uniforms, despite the French having also suffered heavy losses. Napoleon's face is majestic as in the previous portraits.

❧

Claire Elisabeth de Rémusat, in speaking of this picture in her Mémoires, notes the general's inner turmoil: *"A most beautiful painting which portrays him in the middle of the dead and dying as he raises his eye to the sky to seek solace for the horrific scene to which he is witness"*. In addition to paying homage to the great leader, Gros' Napoleon seems to be saying: *"I am the first to ask him why this entails so much suffering, but in the end, I must accept that it is God who has entrusted me with this mission"*. Napoleon told the facts in a reserved manner. This time, however, the tone of the Bulletin de la Grande Armée is one of personal grief and sorrow rather than the usual detached rhetoric. Though the Emperor had been victorious, he did not wish to quantify the number of casualties on the French side. Nevertheless, the Parisians, who were able to read the very few publications which had escaped the clutches of dictatorial censorship, had got wind of a sea change. Despite having killed, wounded or taken prisoner of more than forty thousand enemy troops, Napoleon states: *"Those valiant soldiers who lost their lives on the battlefield did not do so in vain. They died a glorious death as befits true soldiers. We are deeply indebted to both them and their families at whose disposal we shall constantly be and to whom we express our deepest gratitude"*. Some days later, in a letter to the Minister of Police Joseph Fouché, the government runs the risk of making public the terrible toll on the French side: 1500 dead and no fewer than six thousand gravely wounded or injured. There is even the likelihood that these figures had been played down. Regardless of press censorship, the French public are awakening to the true scale of the slaughter, mainly through letters arriving directly from the front, the soldiers' desperate anxiety-filled accounts provoke wide-scale alarm and repugnance. The self-proclaimed glorious victory had been nothing other than a bloody massacre for the majority of the participants. This appalling show had even affected Bonaparte himself to the point that he owned up to his closest collaborators: *"A father who loses his children, does not find any pleasure in victory"*.

1.5 Self Projection

The spin doctors who manage modern election campaigns often point out that a candidate's success depends on a perfect combination between self-image projection, of the identity and moral values the candidates wish to represent and the perceived expectations, needs and passions of the voters. It is not simply tied to their capacity of guaranteeing certain issues. They have to embody a certain lifestyle and class, something which the majority of the electorate can identify with, a standard-bearer for the latters' hopes and aspirations and the spirit of the age. In short, they must capture the Zeitgeist. This is what Napoleon did, long before it became accepted political theory. He used the Revolution as a springboard for greater social opportunities.

It is said that in the army, you can make a career rather than just clinging on for survival. The example that Napoleon gives before he lavishly started handing out rewards as first general, the First Consul then Emperor, was the self-projection of himself. This man of middle-class origin, who deservedly reached the highest echelons of power, became the main player of his age. He is the man who knows everything because he foresees and calculates everything. He can hold forth on any given subject. He takes advantage of the summits at Tilsit and Erfurt to flaunt his vast cultural knowledge. He promotes and modernizes art, making it available to all social classes. He is true to the spirit of 14 July in cleansing age-old hatred and investing in significant social reform. Driven by the belief that it is conviction rather than force that guides men, his philosophy tends to be Sophist rather than Platonic. *"Truth is superfluous, we have to hand out fairy tales for the young and old alike". He is fully aware that: "You cannot lead a people without showing them where the future lies".*

The biggest fairy tale ever told by Bonaparte centres on himself. It rests firmly on indisputable qualities: any tale which is lacking in this would not stand up to the test as the listener would quickly lose interest. This is maintained by the twenty-first century spin doctors.

Napoleon uses his superior skills to shore up an historical period tailor-made for his own use and consumption. It is the tale of a Titan born to reshape Europe along Republican lines. Napoleon domination paid lip-service to the idea of freeing the masses from the yolk of tyranny. The enhancement of culture to the greater glory of his own person is comparable to the emperors of Ancient Rome and smacks of the Machiavellian philosophy "the end justifies the means". This is best shown in the plundering of art treasures in Italy and Egypt which were consigned to The Louvre. Napoleon loves power, but realises that in order to keep it he must never be perceived as a tyrant. This results in him wanting to come across as a man of science and a scholarly warrior rather than a mere fighter. France cannot be commanded by means of an army, he maintains. This is why he does not wish to be perceived as a military dictator. This stance was first taken on at the time of the Egyptian expedition, when he signs his letters: *"Bonaparte, Member of the Institute and Chief of Staff"* giving priority to his intellectual title rather than his military one. His intellectual image never takes second place even when he is commanding his army. Quite the opposite. In the Memorial of Saint Helena written by Emmanuel de Las Cases, it is highlighted how, for the Emperor, it is more important to underline his intellectual attributes to the soldiers rather than his military ones. It is in the intellectual field that he can wield his power rather than in the military one, where he could be equalled and even beaten by an adversary with greater fighting skills and courage. It was not by chance that the old experienced soldier-general Dominique-Joseph Vandamme was forced to admit: *""It happens that I, who fear neither God nor the Devil, start to shake like a leaf when I come up to him".* His intelligence, which was neither lacking in arrogance nor vulgarity, was as if it was magnetic and held everyone in its thrall. It affected both men and women in equal measure.

His culture was based on action which tried to get to the heart of the problem. It was not limited to military science, rather it also extended to the aesthetic and emotional spheres and tried to reduce them to rational mechanisms. His logic is described thus in Friedrich Kircheisen's Memoirs: *"Various topics are stored in my mind like in a wardrobe. When I wish to interrupt a certain thought, I close that particular drawer and open another one. What happens when I want to sleep? I close all the drawers and I immediately drop off"*. It is as if a robot were self-analyzing itself. On the other hand his relationship with knowledge did not give him total intellectual enjoyment". *Reading without a pencil is just dreaming"*. He loves being on the side of the common people. He likes to be seen at the theatre. By talking to the masses, he is able to understand which way the wind is blowing politically. He is able to glean how he is perceived, how he might go about improving his public image. He never does this passively, instead he constantly endeavours to project himself as the protector of the people, the champion of the poor. He does exactly the same regarding the economic situation, religious freedom and the promotion of the arts.

◆

The Achille's heel of the Napoleonic fairy-tale is the desperate need for a happy ending. The Emperor must win, but his battles never finish. His legitimacy is constantly up for renewal and depends on a victory. He acknowledges with a desperate lucidity when writing a letter to the diplomat and politician Klemens von Metternich in June 1813: *"Your kings who were born to the throne can afford to lose twenty consecutive battles and still return to their capital cities. I cannot as I am a simple soldier who has risen through the ranks. My dominion will finish the very day I stop being strong and no longer feared"*.

2

THE WAR OF COMMUNICATION

Swiftness and distribution of information are the two factors essential
to military success. The control, manipulation and instrumentalisation of the
message contribute to the rise and political affirmation of Bonaparte.

2.1 Autonomy of the Army and Integrated Communication

The added value of the relationship of trust set up between Napoleon and his troops (which today we would call paternalistic), was ever present in the efficient carrying-out of orders. The modernization of the army has a fundamental bearing on the flexibility of manoeuvres, the speeding up of displacement exercises, and the capability of swiftly turning round situations. For all this to be successful, both officials and soldiers had to act with a certain degree of autonomy, something which had never happened before in the past. This combination of extra responsibility and duties coupled with successive victories on the battlefield ended up galvanizing the army and making it more cohesive. The soldiers went about their duties happily knowing that they were superior to the enemy and were guided by an invincible general. Communication took on a fundamental role. In this sense, Napoleon was a century and a half ahead of his time, as this way of working is adopted nowadays by the authoritative international association Project Management Institute, whose belief is that 90% of a project manager's work lies in communication.

The Napoleonic army might have been huge and disparate, but it moved as a single unit. The directives given out by The Emperor to one particular corps were also made known to other corps. The development of manoeuvres leading up to a battle, were common knowledge to the whole army. Napoleon had the functional value of the message clear in his mind, knowing full well that the timely delivery of information could facilitate a practicability of the new model flexible army.

When he routs the forces of the Austrian general Karl Mack at Ulm in 1805, he does so by compelling his men to march in forced stages at a brisk pace. By doing this, he was able to avoid being caught up by the Russian army, who was on its way to provide the Austrians with reinforcements. This was all done only after telling his seven armed corps beforehand. The shared awareness of a sense of sacrifice lightened things for him. He calls his foot soldiers grumblers. It is true that they often complain, but they do it in a good-natured way with a touch of humour because deep down they are devoted to the cause of a general who they adore. So, when they say: *"The Emperor has discovered a new way of waging war, he wants us to use our feet instead of our bayonets"*, they are not distancing themselves from their leader, but instead, as their admiration overcomes their fatigue, they are preparing to put his ingenious strategy into action.

The French soldiers have the edge, not only in the physical marching stakes, but they are also better prepared mentally as they constantly know how things are developing and what is required of them. It is not enough to issue an initial briefing and nothing else. Ulm is an example of how fruitful it is to keep the soldiers constantly updated. The changes of track carried out by Napoleon based on information passed on by informers regarding the current state of the battle allow the French army to attain its most optimal position and have the Austrian army surrounded. The outcome of the battle is no longer in doubt. At Ulm it is integrated information which wins the day.

On the enemy's side of the battle, quite the opposite occurred. For as clear and swift as Napoleon's internal intelligence was, the enemy's was just as cumbersome and ineffective. The French state and army were a formidably smooth and streamlined war-machine. The press only reported what Napoleon wanted people to hear. The frontiers are impassable. There is a huge gap between the two armies in terms of intelligence and information. This will be the Austrians' downfall. The gap became significant thanks to the flexibility of the French army. Continued skirmishes and raids throw the enemy into a state of confusion. Austrian spies only receive scraps of information which are actually deceptive and counter-productive. An illustration of this occurs on 16 October 1805, when the Austrians are led to believe that Marshal Jean Lannes' fifth battalion is positioned at Ulm and has been supplemented by two infantry divisions under the respective command of generals Nicolas Oudinot and Honoré Gazan, in addition to a light cavalry led by Jean-Baptiste Treilhard. This was no cause for concern for the Austrians, but little did they know that the fifth battalion had already been strengthened by a further infantry that had detached itself from Michel de Ney's and Augustus de Marmont's divisions, with the further addition of three cavalry divisions which had broken away from the corps led by Joachim Murat. Even these formations would be changed within a matter of days. The effective use of time wins the day. Swiftness of action brings success. This is the one aspect of warfare which Napoleon holds most dear. *"Once time is lost in battle, you will never be able to get it back"* he will go on to say. *"Strategy is the art of making good use of time and distance. Be less thrifty with the latter, distance can be retrieved, time cannot"*.

In contrast to the necessity of carrying out swift and unplanned alterations to the battle-plan within a brief time frame, there is the meticulous planning of the battle itself. Nobody is more familiar with the terrain than the Corsican. Before attempting to access it with his forces, he will spend months poring over it. He wants to leave nothing to chance. It is his expertise in warfare which allows him to be flexible and to issue efficient on-the-spot orders based on prevailing external factors. His extraordinary quick-wittedness affords him the occasion to adopt alternative solutions without excessive pondering.

2.2 Revolutionizing the Concept of Line Formations in the Army

When integrated communication is mentioned in modern companies, this does not just refer to the integration of the various technologies available for transmitting messages (e-mail, social networks, instant messaging), but also the different levels within the company (top management, logistics, marketing, production), both within the company itself and externally. It is in this second sense, regarding his military revolution, that Napoleon foreshadows the adoption of techniques which are today considered to be at the cutting edge in the field of company logistics. Swiftness and efficiency of information were indeed vital for the formation of his troops, which was considered to be revolutionary at the time. Napoleon's far-sighted tactics had nothing to do with those of his enemy, which still adopted inefficient and pedestrian formations from the seventeenth century. Traditional armies, like the one which lined up against the French at Austerlitz, had one single front line without any gaps in it. It advanced relentlessly, firing off volleys of shots at the enemy without any specific target.

On the other hand, the Emperor's regiment was made up of battalions, each constituting two companies standing at a distance of around one hundred and fifty meters from one another. The lighter companies, set up in 1804 by Napoleon after his reform, were known as the skirmishers and they operated in front of the battalions. Napoleon's front line was far more flexible than his enemies'. Moreover, it was capable of covering a far greater amount of territory than the enemy could with the same number of men (furthermore, there were no spaces between the latter's companies). Although the enemy's fire power might have been greater, it was no match for the flexibility of La Grande Armée. The space between one battalion and another allowed both for last minute decisive manoeuvres and for the skirmishers to retreat to the line once they had finished their offensive action as soon as an opportune moment presented itself. It also allowed the artillery to be more effective and for reinforcements to join the lines.

It was space, therefore, which allowed for spur-of-the moment decisions, a luxury which his rigid and compact enemies did not have at their disposal. For a cunning strategist like Bonaparte, this became what is known in the modern company as the competitive edge. It was only possible thanks to a constant to and fro exchange of information which was immediate and efficient. Furthermore, very often, it required his generals to act independently from him and to make decisions on the spot. In this sense, Napoleon, as is underlined by Suchet, is a forerunner of the modern day manager, in as much as he optimizes his resources, by delegating responsibility to his "military line managers".

❧

This happy symbiosis between communication and operational flexibility made even the most complicated solutions possible on the battlefield itself. It was a combination of options which, according to the famous historians Basil Liddel Hart and David Chandler, in their analytical breakdown, works on three levels, as far as the general structuring is concerned. It was then followed by the killer blow. Whenever the French army was engaged against an isolated unit, it adopted the outflanking mode. Its numerical superiority allowed it to face the enemy with just one or two corps (however, by the time his army came to face the Third Coalition, their number had risen to seven). This meant that the rest of the army could form its full flank, and the enemy was totally outflanked, which effectively meant that they were cut off with no means of escape. Furthermore, no information could be conveyed. Outflanking had various uses depending on the situation. It could be carried out by an external corps in support of the main unit, or it could be the work of a specialized formation which broke off from the main unit in order to catch the enemy off guard, or to unsettle and compel them to change formation. The basic idea behind it was to cause both psychological and physical disarray within enemy ranks, through surprise attacks which caught them off guard, weakened their formations, and forced them to defend themselves from a disadvantageous position where their flanks were exposed. As far as outcomes were concerned, the opening of an attack front usually resulted in providing a victory, while skirmishing brought about positional advantages which were mostly short-term. The "wedge" was Bonaparte's preferred tactic when having to face two armies simultaneously. His army concentrated their assaults against the allied troops' weakest link. Once their position had been consolidated, a small part of Napoleon's army stood up to one part of the enemy, while the remaining bigger part routed the rest. This would be followed by moving over to the other flank, aided by the cavalry to help the smaller units of their fellow soldiers which had so far taken the brunt of the enemy assaults.

⁓

This strategy of penetration was drawn up to pierce an extended enemy line containing an excessive number of soldiers. This is how the French army broke through the enemy lines in order to take up a new position or even a nearby town, from where it would have been possible to re-organize, regroup and optimize fighting conditions for the struggle which lay ahead.

Regardless of what had been prepared before, the coup de force, as the French call it (killer blow or knock-out punch), was the decisive moment, where all available fire power ranging from the infantry and the artillery through to the cavalry was brought into play. One of Napoleon's favourite sayings was: *"The best form of defence is attack"*. This is true in matters such as sports and takes on an almost trivial and tragic aspect when applied to sport, rather than the more complex and dangerous activity of warfare. It cannot be denied, however, that Bonaparte's great skill in achieving so many triumphs has brought about many schools of thought and his strategic skills have taken on mythical proportions.

The French collectively look back fondly on Napoleon's greatness and glorious triumphs in order to seek solace after the humiliating defeats of 1870. Remembering his great exploits and achievements was a way of overcoming the humiliation of the recent setbacks and an attempt to bolster flagging national spirit.

Our hero's genius, which is now held in universal esteem by memoir writers from every part of the world, and has overcome the smear campaign run by the British government during his final glory years and those of subsequent decline, has inspired scholars of military strategy worldwide to emulate him.

The French and the Germans attempted to partially adopt Napoleon's battlefield tactics at the outset of the First World War, only for both sides to abandon them after realising that these tactics were not compatible with the technology of the time, which ranged from automatic machine guns to barbed-wire. Although his tactics had helped to achieve so much success a little over a century before, this time round, they only resulted in bloodshed and a pointless waste of life.

A comparison with the Great War can help us understand how it was possible for Napoleon, not taking into account the technical efficiency of his warfare, to maintain a smooth relationship with his soldiers despite the terrible toll sustaned in no less than sixty battles. The frightening yet clear figures tell it all. The death toll amongst the French in the First World War roughly numbered 1.360.000 men. This represents a yearly average of 340.000 victims between 1914 and 1918. The number of men lost in Napoleon's armies is unclear and open to question. Various estimates put it at between 450.000 and 1.500.000, over a longer time span of eleven years. Hence, in the worst case scenario, an average number of 136.000 soldiers fell each year. A blood-curdling toll indeed which reveals however, how accurate this figure was. The reader must take into consideration how much worse life conditions were in Napoleonic times and that soldiers were more willing to put their already precarious lives at stake in order to maintain the Napoleonic legend.

2.3 Egypt: Clutching Victory from the Jaws of Defeat

"Just what is propaganda, if not the attempt to alter people's perceptions and to replace one social model with another?". This rhetorical question was posed by American journalist and essayist, Walter Lippmann, (his "Public Opinion" has, in the meantime, become a "Style Bible") and was put into practice a century earlier by the legendary Corsican. The art of turning the tables to your own advantage is breathtakingly carried out during general Bonaparte's expedition to Egypt. The purpose of the mission set out by The Directory was evident: Egypt was the starting point from which to subsequently hit British interests in India: this could be done by conquering one of the British Empire's most important North African power bases and a staging post to their greatest colonial treasure. The idea was brought forward with great enthusiasm by the very same Napoleon who strongly believed it was necessary to finance and structure an expedition in the Mediterranean. Conquering Egypt, the Corsican explained, meant weakening British power and choking off trade routes towards India, and even making it virtually impossible to maintain contact with its treasured colony. Napoleon fell short of his objective after his initial successes: the Battle of the Pyramids, the defeat of the Mameluch at Mured Bey and the triumphal entry into Cairo. The French fleet was then annihilated by its numerically inferior British counterpart led by the Admiral Horatio Nelson. The ease with which Nelson turned the tables was the litmus test that showed the Egyptian Expedition had been superficially planned. At the time, the British fleet was so superior to any other European counterpart that it is hard to believe the French did not take this into consideration before foolhardily embarking on this expedition. Being unable to obtain new supplies, Napoleon found himself ensnared in a dilemma which the British forecast with rash optimism. Rather than the British, it was he who was totally cut off from the homeland.

On the other hand, the ease with which he was granted the go-ahead is a further indication of just how weak the French government was. At the time, Napoleon's fame had become a source of discomfort for The Directory. In order to get him from under their feet, they were more than happy to acquiesce to his designs. Just as long as these designs were military rather than political in nature, and Paris was able to keep him far from the political power bases, any excuse was good enough to remove a potential political rival from the seat of power. After the drubbing of the French fleet, Napoleon tries in vain to conquer Syria. In the end, it turned out to be a disastrous campaign which lasted two months. The land victory at Abukir, in which Napoleon subdued roughly ten thousand Ottomans under the command of Mustafa Pascià, provided scant consolation for the general, a year after the naval debacle. Bonaparte, well aware of the eventual negative results of a siege at St John of Acre in which his troops were decimated by disease, finally came to terms with the futility of continuing the mission.It is at this point that Napoleon's lucid cynical and equally ingenious ability to interpret the facts comes to the fore. He takes stock of the situation and makes the right move at the right time. What should he do in this situation? Give up on the mission and retreat with his army? This would have been a disastrous move. The British, having total control of the Mediterranean could have slaughtered the entire expedition army. Furthermore, should they miraculously make it back to France, avoiding annihilation, the consequences of failure would have to be accounted for. Politics and image. All the blame would fall exclusively at Napoleon's door. Our man chooses the third way. He leaves the army under the command of general Jean-Baptiste Kléber and boards ship alone to sail back to the homeland. This decision, which was taken in August 1799, leaves Kleber dumbfounded, along with many other high-ranking officers of the eastern army. Bonaparte summons the general to Rosetta in order to debrief him. The Corsican, however, does not show up, leaving instead a dossier which, paradoxically, contains instructions to prepare for swift repatriation of some of his most faithful officers, with General Desaix being at the top of the list. In short, Kleber is left to *"mind the garbage"* having been put in the impossible position of having to do better than when the army was at full strength.

Always paying full attention to the delicate balances of communication, Napoleon leaves his military successors the task of making his proclamation known to the Muslim èlite of Cairo, in which he shamelessly pretends to want to return to Egypt three months later, hence giving him the time he needs to *"deal a blow which will see off all his enemies in one fell swoop"*.

In reality, Bonaparte knows full well the psychological effect of the news of his departure will not take long to make its mark on the ruling class of this country and particularly on his detractors. His promise of a swift return is only a smokescreen in order to buy himself more time to organize the French resistance against likely new attacks from a revitalized enemy. As far as his troops are concerned, Napoleon will sacrifice a great many of them who followed him unconditionally, due to their veneration for him, simply for the sake of his lust for power. With the benefit of hindsight, his address to them to mark their conquest of Egypt: *"Forty centuries of history now look down on you from the top of this pyramid"* now seems to mock them. The messages, proclamations and promises are simply a way of achieving immediate objectives, which are often tactical. They have remained valid over time due to political and personal interest. Although the general's image had suffered a relapse in some of his soldiers' eyes, as was inevitable in the Egyptian affair, the assessment of whether to retreat or not was made exclusively on the basis of a lucid, and perhaps even cynical, self-interest. Given the political state of affairs, Napoleon seems justified in making the choices he did. Territories which had been gained in Italy had nearly all been repossessed by the anti-French coalition. The French general Barthélemy Scherer retreats towards Piedmont, while his counterpart, Jean Victor Moreau, is forced to give up Milan. Jean-Baptiste Jourdan, routed at Stockach, retreats towards the Rhine. The Directory is on its knees, crushed by military defeats, economic downturn and a growing nostalgia amongst many for the Ancien Régime.

The truth is that the depletion of the Italian garrisons of troupes caused by the Egyptian campaign played an important role in helping the second anti-French coalition win the day. However, public opinion perceives something entirely different, and this is true in part; the fact that the Corsican's military leadership is far superior to that of the man who has replaced him in the Iberian Peninsula. Furthermore, in France, the semi-disaster that was the Egyptian campaign, has served to bolster Napoleon's reputation. With his usual ingenious intuition, from the very outset, this expedition was given a meaning far beyond a simple military one. It was extended to take in scholarly and archaeological needs. Betting on the colonization of a region with a millennium old culture turned out to be a winning card. From the Rosetta Stone through to other archaeological finds, the mission was no longer conceived as a military by the general public, but rather a cultural and educational one. These were the new values of progress delivered by the revolution and safeguarded by the general's growing legend, which were being exported abroad. These messages spring, first and foremost, from the man's extraordinary capacity for communication. He was able to bring great moments from mythology back to life. He was even able to account for his failure in Egypt as an heroic failure, an expedition led by an invincible leader doomed from the very start, along the lines of the Greek mythological saying: *"Those the Gods love, they punish"*. His obsession with information and the desire to have complete control over it, led him to have a printing press brought over to North Africa in order to print the new publication titled: 'Courrier de l'Egypte'.

$$\bullet$$

Bonaparte's strategies are never random or concocted on the spot. They are the fruit of careful and meticulous forward planning, as is the case with Egypt. Prior to the campaign, he dedicated much time to careful study of its history, territory, and past and present civilization. Once intellectually armed, he launched his plan of action. Napoleon reads the Koran, emerges himself in the customs of the local people, and even alters his style of dress accordingly to fit in with the local people. His marketing and communication campaign, which was managed in France by his brother Lucien, was also developed in the occupied territory. He wanted to give out a reassuring signal to the natives, to show them that France was a peaceful progressive nation committed to bringing social justice rather than merely invading and colonizing their land. This is consistent with his cold, lucid political vision and foreshadows the 18 Brumaire.

The failed siege of St John of Acre and all its dramatic implications will have to be faced up to by those who are forced to remain on the field of combat. While, for Napoleon, there is only widespread praise and respect.

When he decides to abandon Egypt, he has not been sanctioned to do so by The Directory. Some members of the post-revolutionary government, however, have already envisaged the necessity to call him back to the homeland, as it is he, more than any other, who is capable of reining in and turning round a situation which looks set to become a military debacle.

The Corsican beats them to it, by turning up uninvited at their command centre. The weakness of this governmental body is best described by Stendhal in a footnote in his "Life of Napoleon" by explaining how the issue of Napoleon's disobedience was dealt with *"Upon receiving news of Bonaparte's return to France, the Directory gave Fouché, who was then the Minister of Police, a warrant to arrest him. That well-known traitor replied: "He is not a man to be arrested. Nor shall I be the man to arrest him".* Napoleon lands in Provence on 21 Vendémiaire and the whole country soon knows about it and rejoices at the return of their great military leader. He takes up residence in Paris and endeavours to bolster the cultural aspect of his recent expedition. He even goes as far as giving lectures at L'Institut de France. In short, he is ready to wear the mantle of the leading figure in a new era of post-revolutionary France.

2.4 The Role of Lucien and the Value of Freedom

Turning somebody into a living legend tends, amongst other things, to underline and bolster the person's merits, just as a fall from grace has the opposite effect and it magnifies faults and weaknesses. In the growing collective French public opinion, 18 Brumiaire 1799 marked the umpteenth direct hit of a genius who knew just how to combine the skill of a great military leader with the rhetorical finesse of a great statesman; just as a master chess player is able to foresee his opponent's moves and is able to outwit him thanks to his own farsightedness.

Indeed, despite The Directory's weakness, nobody was in a position to be certain of the success of the coup d'état that Bonaparte and his allies were planning. There was a further complication. Of the three consuls who had taken on power, the one who had dreamt up the plan for the coup was Sieyès. He harboured ambitions to be the leader of France, since he considered himself to have far greater political acumen and experience than his two partners in crime.

The overwhelming success of the operation and the subsequent appointment of Napoleon as First Consul and effective leader of a state which was shedding its republican ideals, bear witness to Napoleon's incredible skill at turning everything to his advantage, in addition to always coming out on top in any situation. These were natural talents which were typical of the superman to whom, very shortly, the majority of the population would willingly hand over the reins of power. When looking closely at the mechanisms which brought the Corsican to power, the important role played by his brother Lucien is plain to see. Thanks to the whim of Sieyès, he had been appointed as an important member of the previous government. He was appointed as the president of The Council of the Five Hundred, one of two branches of the Parliament. The unlikely uprising of the elusive anarchists and Napoleon's appointment as the commander of the Parisian garrison were the prelude which brought about the resignation of high-ranking Directory leaders such as Emmanuel Sieyès and Paul Barras.

⁂

The proposal of a Consulate to serve The Republic as a safeguard against any future uprisings was brought up by Napoleon himself on 19 brumaire in front of a Council of Elders. The council was sceptical and far from convinced of the threat mentioned in his claims. On this occasion, and even more so in dealing with the Council of the Five Hundred, which contained a high number of Jacobin members, Napoleon's communication skills frequently wavered. Having come up against the high-flown political jargon of The Chamber, and having been accused by the Council of the Five Hundred of wanting to carry out an illicit undertaking, Napoleon showed signs of insecurity which had never been seen before. He even started to stammer, probably due to paucity of the arguments he was putting forward.

It is true that Napoleon was addressing his detractors, thus opening himself up to his natural opponents and asking them to step down and relinquish their power-base. It is also true that his oratorical shortcomings and his bashfulness in front of his republican opponents probably represent a one-off failure; nevertheless, it was a complete defeat. However, it was only momentary and of no subsequent significance. Just as indisputable, in the face of his brother's uncertainty, was the lucidity and swiftness with which Lucien acted when asked to back a motion which would declare Napoleon an outlaw. Rather than backing it and effectively letting Robespierre send his own flesh and blood to the guillotine, he refused outright and suspended Parliament. He then called in the garrison to deal with turbulent politicians. It was the right move and had certainly been planned beforehand whilst setting up the plot. However, it was carried out with a determination and presence of mind, two qualities which Bonaparte, in complete contrast to his character, had failed to show on that particular day. His poor showing on the day was probably brought on by the tension underlying his ambitions to change and rewrite history. Simply put, there was so much at stake, and for once, the situation got the better of him. As his faithful secretary Bourienne writes in his "Memoirs" on the eve of his address to the two chambers, Bonaparte took his leave of him thus: *"This evening we will either sleep at Les Tuileries or we will go to the guillotine"*.

Naturally, Lucien's great skill lays in the ability to make what has been discussed a reality. Bonaparte's rise to the top is owed not only to his great strategic skills, but also to a happy combination of interests which sought to find a solution to the political instability of post-revolutionary France. The astute Talleyrand, who was one of the plotters of 18 brumiaire, had begun to take a close interest in the issue from August 1879 onwards, when he expressed his desire for The Directory to be replaced with a military political body. In his view, the army was the guardian angel of the French state. While the new institutions had partly failed, the power of the sword had not. It had been the army which had prevented the nation from being handed over to a foreign power after the disastrous civil war. It was the last bastion upon which a new trust could be built in order to build strong governance. It was the middle ground between an eventual Legitimist vendetta and Jacobin revanchism. There seemed to be no other alternatives given the way recent historical events had turned out. Napoleon, the new man and outsider, grasped the opportunity given to him by the tide of history and rode his "luck" in the Machiavellian sense of the word. The end of the Revolution obviously brought with it limitations to freedom of expression. As he explains in his own inimitable way in his "Memoirs of Saint Helena", the defence of physical national boundaries meant setting up personal ones in the shape of restrictions. Thiers states in his paradoxical analysis (Adolphe Thiers, "Storia della Rivoluzione francese", Milano, Dall'Oglio, 1963) that it is the suppression of rights which transforms itself into a liberating device: *"The revolution which was supposed to give France freedom and was planned in such a way as to give it to her was not and should not have been about freedom itself, It should have been a struggle to overcome the old order. After it had been crushed in France, the logical progression was to bring it down in Europe too. Such a violent struggle however had nothing to do with freedom, neither in shape nor spirit".* Napoleon's solution however, as Luigi Mascilli Migliorini reveals, left two knots untied. To the more astute thinkers of the time, these two knots should have been unravelled in order to unblock the impasse created by the revolution: peace and the definition of forms or representation.

This failure was anything but negligible. Napoleon, however, was fully aware of the importance of putting himself across to the masses as a champion of freedom. His operation only reaches its apex, as we will see, when he is on Saint Helena, because he has been totally shorn of power and his life is coming to an end. Yet, he had done it before. Thiers' interpretation is over-romanticised, because as Mascilli Migliorini points out, he views the great Corsican as a legend, wielding his sword against the strongholds of the conservatism of the Ancien Régime. This is how such great cultural giants as Goethe, Alessandro Manzoni, Ludwig van Beethoven, and Johann Fichte romantically viewed him. Even Friedrich Hegel went as far to define him as "The living embodiment of world spirit". Even those who pointed out his faults ended up being dazzled by his legend, thus falling into the same trap. For example, the father of French romanticism, the diplomat and writer, Francois-René de Chateubriand, praises him thus: *"A poet in action, a great genius of warfare, an untiring spirit, a wise and able administrator, a committed and reasonable legislator".*

⁂

For Napoleon, beyond the self-obsessed self-projection of his glorious and triumphal fifteen years at the top until his downfall at Saint Helena, political freedom remained nothing more than: *"A conventional fairy-tale made up by governments in order to deceive the governed".* He goes further to state that: *"Good politics means fooling the people into thinking they are free and making them feel happy"".* In this game of charades, where ideals are cynically waved around under the banner of a new social pact, formed by a wide umbrella group representing the various members of the vast third estate and their conflicting demands, the line between story-telling and true fact becomes blurred if not indistinguishable. *"Historical truth is a fairy tale"* is another of Bonaparte's famous aphorisms Another instance in which Napoleon showed both ignominiously and contradictorily that he preferred rigid state law over freedom was in 1802 when the historical yet illusory Peace of Amiens was signed with Great Britain. In order to avoid discriminatory regimes between colonies already in

French possession and those ceded by the British following the treaty, the First Consul could find no better solution than to reintroduce slavery, so as not to upset the new white masters of the newly acquired territories who had put him under pressure. The people of these newly acquired colonies were clear in expressing their preference for the former British rule who had stipulated at the time of the handover that the natives were not to be exploited and slave-trading was forbidden. The heir of the Revolution decreed a return to the past for these lands which had undergone progressive reform and had obtained statutory basic human rights. It would all end in tears, as thousands of rebellious ex-slaves would be massacred in the West Indies and particularly in Santo Domingo.

2.5 The Stolen Victory

It was Amedeo Lavy, the sculptor, engraver and medal maker from Turin, who minted the golden Marengo, the famous coin which bore the image of Napoleon; first as First Consul and later as Emperor. Furthermore, it was intended to bear historic witness to the Subalpine Republic. Millions of these 20 franc coins were also minted on the French side of The Alps. Marengo-Napoleon is a pairing which evokes the legendary victory on 14 June 1800 over the Austrian army led by general Melas. A day later, a summit ratified that the Austrians should retreat to Venice, leaving the rest of Northern Italy to Napoleon and his army. The victory at Marengo was, without a doubt, very important as far as consolidation and expansion of the Republican Army was concerned. The ensuing celebrations were an example of Bonaparte's extraordinary capacity for self-agrandissement. Italy was in thrall to the fascination of the Revolution, its ideals and what it had seemingly brought about. The great men of letters such as Ugo Foscolo and Vincenzo Monti heaped lavish praise upon Bonaparte, who they perceived as a triumphant hero. In the field of art, the adulation was just as fervent. Often commissioned, the paintings of Gros, David and other leading artists of that time, immortalized Napoleon on his second Italian campaign.

Often commissioned, the paintings of Gros, David and other leading artists of that time, immortalized Napoleon on his second Italian campaign. The victory was embellished with many tales and legends. There were even spin-offs such as the "Chicken Marengo", which was supposedly eaten by the great man for the first time the day before the historic battle. Napoleon was happy for all these stories to proliferate, as they would help to bolster his growing legendary status.

Let it be noted however, that at the time of Marengo, the zeitgeist was different to the one at the time of Jena and Austerlitz. The Italian successes were propitious to the army led by the First Consul, who was yet to enjoy the peak of his glory years, when he would enjoy the adulation of his own men and receive universal loathing from his enemies. In the boiling cauldron of post-revolutionary France, those in power followed one another falteringly and ineffectively. Napoleon had already begun to buck this trend. Yet, he was only at the beginning. No-one, including himself, would have ever imagined that he would dominate the European stage for fifteen years. It would not have taken much to overturn this train of events. Just a few years earlier, at the time of Trafalgar and Austerlitz, he had become the universal bogey man. English mothers would threaten their children with the arrival of the monster "Boney" (a mocking diminutive of his name) should they misbehave. Napoleon, therefore, used Marengo as a stepping stone for his relentless ascent to glory. Although the official dispatches and journals poured praise and adulation on his achievements, and played up the importance of his triumph; for him personally, it felt like a defeat.

❧

The timely arrival of reinforcements late in the afternoon of that fateful 14 June is what saved Napoleon from inevitable disaster. The reinforcements consisted of a cluster of five thousand men led by general Louis Charles Antoine Desaix, Bonaparte's brave and valiant friend. Along with the help of a weary but heroic and weakened cavalry led by general Francois Kellermann, the tables were miraculously turned on a battlefield from which the French army had all but decided to retreat. Desaix would not come out of the conflict alive. The other protagonists of this magical victory, such as generals Jean Lannes and Claude-Victor Perrin, would be rewarded a few years later with the appointment of Marshall. Bonaparte's great skill in holding everything together and in creating a team spirit will ensure that there will be no criticisms or rebukes in the press reports following the victory. If there was one person who did not deserve to claim the title of winner at Marengo, it was Napoleon himself. He had been guilty of recklessness when he split his up men up and told Desaix to head with his division towards Genoa in order to prevent the Austrians from joining up with the British fleet. He only called him back at 1 p.m. on 14 June, after the situation had become desperate. During the battle, he remained uncharacteristically passive and listless. Furthermore, he retreated to his quarters, which were so far off from the scene of battle that it only seemed to give Melas the upper-hand and an inevitable victory. Every great general is entitled to an off-day and 14 June 1800 at Marengo was Napoleon's. It seemed it would come back to haunt him. So much so, that general Melas just before the timely arrival of Desaix, was heading for Alessandria to hand in the dispatch claiming victory. Overconfidence, in addition to the slowness with which the Austrians pursued their French adversaries, due to the fact they were on a plundering mission, resulted in the French gaining the necessary time for Desaix and his men to arrive and save the day. The heroism of several generals and their divisions, such as the one led by general Francois Kellermann, transformed certain defeat into victory. However, the subsequent praise and adulation in the form of written word or paintings gives Napoleon all the credit. This did not happen by chance. It was brought about by the First Consul's wisdom, lucidity, and cynicism which helped him to fully exploit the gift that fate had kindly thrown at his feet.

2.6 The Russian Campaign and its Dispatches

When we speak of a war of communication, nothing is more exemplary than the strategy used in a real war, none more so than that adopted in the war to end all wars; the Russian campaign.

It is 1812. Only a few years earlier in Erfurt, when Napoleon and Alexander I of Russia met up on such friendly terms, nobody could have envisaged such a gruesome turn-around in the relationship between the two Empires. In reality, the Tsar had sought a friendly and diplomatic solution to the French issue. Although the climate was superficially peaceful and portentous to achieving this, actual conditions were not conducive to bringing about a long-lasting peace between the two super powers. The fact of having to join the Continental Blockade against The British, ran contrary to Russian interests, while their economy was badly affected as a result. Furthermore, in an attempt to bolster the Grand Alliance, Bonaparte sought to take yet another Tsar's sister's hand in marriage, which would create a new geo-political dynasty and bring the Bonapartes within the orbit of the great royal and imperial families. This was not only met with fierce opposition by Alexander, who it seems had initially entertained the idea, but also by his wife and the Russian aristocracy. This abrupt political volte-face towards France on the Tsar's part, which was manifested in Russia's withdrawal from the Continental Blockade and the resumption of trade with Great Britain, picked up pace when Napoleon decided to seize the German Grand Duchy of Oldenbourg, whose ruler had married one of the Tsar's sisters. The emperor had decided to act so as to bolster the effect and maintain the smooth running of the anti-British embargo. However this move had the opposite effect on Tsar Alexander, who had run out of patience with Bonaparte, and now considered him unreliable. Within a few months, the political landscape had been turned upside down. Bonaparte was now determined to deliver a decisive blow to his former ally. War operations began in May 1812. As already mentioned, this war would be characterized by its communication's offensive. Its outcomes are sensationally reported in the dispatches of the Grande Armée.

The exactitude of the reports are a matter of conjecture as they were printed in Le Moniteur, the official organ of the dictatorial regime. Attentive reading between the lines would indicate that a lot of the information is inexact, if not downright bogus. First of all, let us consider the timeframe. Up to the point where the Great Army advances and the Russian army, under the command of Mikhail Kutuzov, who would subsequently be immortalized in 'War and Peace', retreats, one dispatch follows another. No less than 18 dispatches are issued by the Emperor from 20 June up to 7 September. They talk of successful missions, of land confiscated from the Tsar. It all seems to be mounting up to a resounding historic victory. Up to the taking of Moscow, the dispatches issued by the Corsican more or less mirror the truth. The mendacious ones are those that follow. An emblematic episode is the false information relayed by the British diplomat in Russia, Wilson, who speaks of a victory for the Russian army at Borodin. In Great Britain, where there is almost total freedom of the press unlike in France, this deceit does not last long. As soon as news is received of the French troops entering Moscow, a prestigious publication, 'The New Statesman', publishes an article brimming with indignation and concern: *"Here is how things stand in this conflict which is harming Russia and could have terrible consequences for Great Britain. (...) Let us hope our fellow countrymen open their eyes and that the wicked falsehoods to which they have been subjected are, in the future, backed up by hard facts"*.

The wheel of fate turns against the French army and the frequency of official dispatches diminishes as the retreat begins. The more the decision to retreat becomes inevitable, the heavier it lies on the Emperor. In making this decision, he is fully aware of the symbolic consequences of his choice. As Dumas will write with his customary astuteness. *"He hesitates and alternatively turns his eye towards Paris, then towards Saint Petersburg. One hundred and fifty leagues separate him from one, eight hundred from the other. Marching on Saint Petersburg will seal his victory, a humiliating return to Paris is tantamount to confessing defeat"*.

Only five dispatches will subsequently be issued in the course of the tragic event which will see France's five to six thousand men brutally halved. The emperor's style is chilling, as he tries to deflect attention from the rout by mentioning the loss of three thousand horses in dispatch 28. They were not horses but men, however the Emperor's main concern is to play down the scale of the tragedy in order not to stir up unnecessary anxiety. He is playing for time before his unwanted but increasingly inevitable return to the homeland. He gives reassurances of his own state of health in Dispatch 29. It is strategically essential that everyone is aware of his survival, as this fact was put in doubt by general Malet, and who on this basis, on 23 October, planned a sort of *coup d'état* as part of the general strategy. The negative effects of this are not long in coming. For the first time ever, Napoleon is seen in a negative light by the masses within the boundaries of France. The 1813 conscription, which calls to arms no fewer than 963 thousand men, sets off a wave of satire, one example of which is a cartoon which portrays Napoleon as an evil ogre feeding year by year on his young sons. This is the beginning of the end for the Corsican. The leading minds of the day are savage in their criticism of him, and he will be overwhelmed by their invective once he has fallen from grace. His first notable detractor was the writer Madame de Stael. Regarding his callousness, she expressed herself thus in her work: "Reflections on the Main Events of the French Revolution", written in 1818: He is neither good, nor violent, nor sweet nor cruel in the way individuals usually are. Such a person, having nothing in common with his fellow man, could neither feel nor inspire fellow feeling. He is both above and below all other men. He regards other human beings as numbers or things not as an equal. Just as he does not love, neither does he hate. For him there is only himself; everybody else on the planet is a mere number, of no consequence whatsoever. We are now suspending belief. How can we deny the charm and the feeling of empathy? It was the social glue which bound post-revolutionary France created by Napoleon.

—❧—

This type of reaction, a denigration and contempt just as strong as any which existed in Great Britain when he was at the height of his power, is the direct result of Bonaparte's cynicism and erroneous communication during his retreat from Russia. Let it be understood, defeat can generally turn a hero into a villain, but Napoleon is guilty of speeding up his own downfall through his deceit, which brought about an inevitable collapse of his popular consensus.

3
THE CONSENSUS

For the first time, a member of the ruling class takes
into consideration public opinion, how to interact with it,
and how much influence it has for the legitimization of his power.

3.1 The Great Forerunner

Communicating also means taking the pulse of those who are known today as stakeholders. Napoleon did this on every level. He built upwards, beginning with the masses, wanting to make them stakeholders. He institutionalized ways of channelling consensus, just as the Ancient Romans used circuses to forge a bond between the Emperor and the plebs.

One of his initiatives was to widen the franchise to millions of French citizens and to invite them to vote for and endorse, under the new system which had arisen from the Revolution, the coup d'ètat which brought about the creation of the Consulate. The plebiscite with which Napoleon was crowned life Consul was effectively a landslide: three and a half million in favour and only eight thousand against; a significant number achieved through the system of direct democracy implemented by Napoleon. He had a natural feel for what could be perceived as modern in terms of democracy, while at the same time, he had an incredible knack for increasing his popularity amongst the masses. The importance of such methods used to create a bond between the elected and the electors would eventually come to the forefront in the centuries to come. There have been recent examples of this which have captured media attention In Italy. They have taken the form of the American primaries with an Italian twist, in which party members at grass-roots levels can decide which candidate to endorse and which to remove from the race for candidacy. Napoleon was also ahead of his time in personalizing politics. This is a European phenomenon which started in the early twentieth century with the dictatorships of Adolf Hitler and Benito Mussolini and then was followed by charismatic leaders such as the British Prime Ministers Winston Churchill, Margaret Thatcher, and Tony Blair, in addition to the French President De Gaulle (also a general), up to the most recent examples of Barack Obama and Matteo Renzi, and in the recent past Silvio Berlusconi and Nicolas Sarkozy.

It was not enough for Napoleon to lead the Grande Armée; he also tried to be the leading ambassador for all his fellow countrymen. He sought to set up friendships which other great leaders such as Tsar Alexander I, and even tried to set up dynasties through marriage, as he did with the Hasburgs. In an age in which the ruling families had to take stock of what happened, first in 1789, and more so in 1793, things became even more conservative in their governance, to which Napoleon reacted by placing the common man at the centre of everything and the blue blood lobby became insignificant. Rather than adopting a pure and simple return to the archetype leader and mythical hero, he reinvented himself as the modern head of state. Even when he failed to achieve significant results, he never gave up on trying to get his ideas and message across. He moved in every direction and used everything he had at his disposal. Even during war.

Many of his dispatches teem with his concern for creating a favourable climate with the people of the territories he coveted. Reading them now, it is astonishing how in synch they are with modern-day diplomacy, as he endeavours to debrief his troops. Two days before landing in Egypt, while his men were aboard the warship "Oriente", his dispatch is handed out to his men and it instructs them on how to interact with the locals. He warns them not to indulge in crime and most importantly to show tolerance at all times: *"The people with whom we shall spend our time are Muslims. Their basic belief is this: there is no other God but Allah and Mohammed is his prophet. Do not contradict them. Behave as you did with the Jews and the Italians. Show respect for their religious customs and their imams, as you did for the rabbis and the bishops (...). The Roman legions protected all religions. Here you will find customs which are different from those in Europe. Endeavour to get used to them. They treat their women differently from how we do. Always remember, he who uses violence is considered a monster".*
This is Napoleon's approach to leading both soldiers and civilians. It is a vision which, despite wavering from time to time for tactical reasons, is extraordinarily modern. His desire to put the spotlight on the people is just as strong as the determination with which he faces his enemies in battle.

Some years later, when he is Prime Consul, he will attempt the same approach with Great Britain, the same enemy against whom he will subsequently enforce The Continental Blockade. His Christmas wishes and the proposal of a «general reconciliation» put forward to George III will not have the desired effect.

Likewise, the Peace of Amiens popular with both the French and the British, will turn out to be a short-lived and unworkable failure. His endeavours to obtain understanding, legitimacy and consensus both at home and abroad aimed at every possible stakeholder ranging from his fellow countrymen to actual and potential enemies, give further evidence of his striking ability, initially as First Consul, then as Emperor, to seek dialogue with and the approval of those he addressed within the framework of his power policy, which was tied to the re-straints of the historical period in which he operated. His constant quest for consensus, both domestic and foreign, did not stop him, however, from lucidly analysing the reality and the often fleeting consistency of the pacts which were reached. This happens to him immediately after signing the agreement in Am-iens. *"A spirit of hostility will always exist between the old monarchies and the newly-founded republics. As things stand today, any peace treaty will only result in a short-lived armistice. I believe my destiny is to fight on incessantly"*.

Objective reasons form the basis for this situation of enforced belligerence. The driving force behind the Revolution, of which Napoleonic France is the stand-ard-bearer, is the quest to unseat the remaining European monarchies. This deep-rooted desire for social change had simmered, come to the surface and spread to the rest of Europe. Nineteenth Century libertarian and egalitarian principals could not have spring up overnight as if by magic; they had to be imposed and Napoleon was prepared to do this. It is clear that the Corsican's character was not one which favoured diplomatic solutions. Upon conquering any given state, he imposed conditions which reduced it to the role of a mere satellite. It had to supply men for his ever-growing army, and unwillingly par-ticipate in embargos and replenish French coffers so Napoleon could continue his war effort against Great Britain, which he never managed to fully subdue. These satellite states would, over the medium-term period, be economically drained without even realising it. It would seem that even without Napoleon, Europe would have been stricken by bloodbaths and slaughter in this period, though it could be argued that Bonaparte, due to his combative nature, ensured that the final toll was even higher. Soon, his insistence on placing conquered states under French hegemony came back to haunt him. It was not long before the occupied people discovered the so-called bringers of freedom for what they really were, a force which merely paid lip-service to the ideals of popular revolution in order to exploit it for their own imperial expansionist aims.

3.2 The Great French Dream: The Legion Of Honour

Napoleon sold a dream. The lives of all French people, be they those who excelled on the battlefield or in civilian life, could be changed for the better.
Social mobility was not impossible; quite the opposite. If certain conditions could be met, he, Bonaparte, would ensure the deserved reward. Progress was not just measured in tangible goods alone. It could also be granted symbolically. A French citizen's social standing could be elevated by the awarding of a special honour. The Legion of Honour, a five-pointed medal attached to a ribbon, was created for this very purpose. The Legion of Honour was an innovative award in as much that it did not carry the usual meaning of state honours in which the recipient is deemed to be superior and effectively distances himself from the masses. The Legion of Honour is radically different due to the fact that it celebrates a person's worth rather than their social class. Up to this point, a state honour marked the recipient's perceived social superiority and was basically an old boys' network of nobles based on nothing more than mutual back-scratching. Napoleon, however, implemented a system where the award was based on parameters strictly connected to merit. It was initially awarded for military merit and was then extended to the civilian field. It was not simply a cosmetic exercise as its recipients gained renown, and the award itself was taken up by governments beyond France.

Although the Legion of Honour might have seemed a meaningless sop, it was consistent with the ideals of the Revolution. It was a symbol of the new meritocracy where everyone had the same rights and possibilities of social advancement through individual merit rather than through birth. The paradox of Napoleon lies in the fact that he not only makes the revolution a reality, but he also simultaneously brings it to an end. His dictatorship slowly replaces the young chaotic republic institutionally without the masses even realizing it. The placing of power in the hands of one man, given the historical context and conditions in France at the time, paradoxically results in the opportunity of real social advancement, both for the middle classes and the lower ones. In reality, the beneficiaries were relatively few, however the perceived improvement in terms of social justice was a driving force which swept away the rigid class system and drove a stake through the heart of the Ancien Regime, which was effectively consigned to the dustbin of history. In his ruthless and efficient drive to modernise France, Napoleon introduced new instruments and innovations such as the Legion of Honour, but he never lost sight of the usefulness of traditional symbolism. He avoided making France completely middle class, thus keeping certain privileges aside for those who were effectively the "chosen few". It was no longer a question of the blood you were born with which made you important, but rather the blood you were prepared to shed on the battlefield in the cause of the new France. The new nobles were his valiant soldiers.

While we are on the subject of blood, perhaps the most important was that which was shed by the enemy upon the various battlefields of Europe. This was the icing on the cake which provided the perfect finishing touch to efficient administration, new social reforms and honours. It symbolized the superiority of Napoleon's new France. This kept the dream alive throughout his near fifteen years of total domination in Europe. From the outset of his dictatorship, this was Napoleon's policy. Even as Prime Consul, when he attempted to make the peace with Austria and Great Britain, he was only paying lip service to the concept. He knew that these two nations would like to see the monarchy reinstated in France, an unacceptable condition which ran contrary to his and the new France's interests. He drew the logical conclusion that a return to armed conflict was inevitable. Fully confident of his military prowess, and knowing he had both the army and the citizens behind him, he filled his soldiers in on exactly what was happening. This was no time for a truce! France was preparing its attack. In his Christmas Day proclamation of 1799, just a few weeks after the Coup d'État, the First Consul addresses his troops *"Soldiers, it is no longer enough to defend our national boundaries. We must invade the enemy states"*. They set off towards new conquests. The Republican dream became reality on foreign soil shored up by the countless number of slaughtered enemy corpses.

3.3 The High Profile Fairy-Tale Wedding

His marriage to Mary Louise of Austria was part of a drive to consolidate his influence and power through inter-personal relationships in addition to that won on the battlefield. Napoleon ably exploited the opportunities offered by this high-profile wedding as a communications exercise. This marriage worked on many communication levels. First of all, the union of the former Prime Consul to the daughter of an Emperor was a clear message to the international community. Franz I's daughter was being married to a middle-class general, who in his turn had become an emperor thanks to his military deeds and exploits rather than by birthright. The Hasburgs of Austria, whose army had been defeated yet again at Wagram by the French army, had to cede a substantial amount of territory under the Peace of Schönbrunn. Furthermore, they were forced to acknowledge the French victor as their social equal. It was Franz himself, alongside his counsellor, Klemens Wenzel von Metternich, who handed the eighteen-year-old imperial scion over to Bonaparte. The latter was the Austrian equivalent of Richelieu, an astute diplomat and politician who would become State Chancellor in 1821. Bonaparte made sure that the marriage created ripples throughout Europe. The civil marriage took place on 1 April 1810 in the Chateau Saint-Cloud. This was a symbolic choice, as it was from there that first the Coup d'Etat of brumiaire 1799 was orchestrated, then a couple of years later Bonaparte declared himself Emperor from the very same place. The religious ceremony was officiated by his uncle, Cardinal Joseph Fesch, the following day; first at the Imperial Palace des Tuileries, then at the Salon Carré du Louvre, which had been transformed into a chapel for the occasion. At the subsequent banquet at Les Tuileries, the newly-weds took to the balcony to salute the celebrating crowd.

Great care was given over to recording the event. The French painter, George Rouget, was called upon to capture the ceremony at The Louvre on canvas. Both the secular and religious ceremonies were solemnly commemorated with the issuing of medals, which were coined by Luigi Manfredini and examples of which can now be found in the Lombardi Museum belonging to the Monteparma Foundation. Even today, memorabilia of Marie Louise is a thriving tourist business in Parma. Even on the occasion of his second wedding, Napoleon was ahead of his time, both in pushing merchandise related to it and claiming the world spotlight. This second wedding could be considered the first ever big media event. It would be echoed at the end of the following century by the so-called high-profile "fairy-tale" wedding, the best example of which is the one between Charles and Diana in 1981. This wedding was broadcast live to over 750 million viewers at a cost of roughly 63 million euros. The Japanese also staged a similar event when Crown Prince Naruhito took the high-flying business woman as his bride. The latter wore a 12 kilo kimono for this special occasion.

3.4 Cultural Paternalism

In carefully building his public image, Napoleon wanted to project himself as the embodiment of the social conquests of the Revolution. The end of domestic conflict sprang from his ambivalence. He was what the Americans would nowadays call: "an ordinary Joe", who was both in tune with the people and knew what they wanted, yet at the same time, he was an invincible and untouchable leader when it came to implementing policies. Whenever he stepped down from his pedestal, culture blossomed and thrived. The Louvre is an example of this. The fame of the Muséum Central des Arts had spread worldwide thanks to the acquisition of many masterpieces which had effectively been pillaged during the Corsican's Italian campaign and subsequently brought back to Paris in 1798. This was all part of the general's and future dictator's grand design, as he was fully aware of the aura which surrounded his person. It was the Prime Consul himself who presided over the inauguration of the most famous masterpieces within the museum's special exhibition rooms. Once again, he was ahead of his time in appointing Vivant Denon as Director of Culture in order to enhance the museum even further. It was no accident that the museum was renamed Musée Napoleon in 1803. It became a symbol of the new middle-class culture, sweeping away the old aristocratic one under the tutelage of its new master.

Culture was enhanced and strengthened by streamlining it to certain directives. The reform of the education system, launched in 1805, was an important building block for this project. Bonaparte extended his cultural reach to the theatre. He was personally involved in handpicking the actors, who had to gain the imperial seal of approval by meeting certain standards. Following a series of decrees issued between 1805 and 1806, the number of theatres in Paris were whittled down to a mere eight, while other towns and cities had to meet stringent standards in order to be able to have a permanent theatre company. This constant attention on Napoleon's part, alongside his pervasive drive and influence within every sphere of life, which sent out messages or created trends, was a power game intended to wipe out feudalism and to simultaneously replace it with a new form of subjection based on middle-class merit instead of aristocratic birth right. In this sense, the new Napoleonic language of power would not be radically different from the old aristocratic one. This is best displayed by the fact that old noble titles did not fall into disuse (prince, duke, count, baron, knight). All these titles were given to those who had distinguished themselves on the battlefield. The old aristocracy has merely been replaced by a limited meritocracy consisting of the privileged few who are able to fulfil the Emperor's wishes, rather than those who showed individual creativity and initiative. The aristocracy, if not completely wiped out, has been decimated. Only those who had great wealth were able to pass on hereditary titles, albeit they were legally bound to stringent laws regarding wealth.

3.5 Censorship and the Instrumentalisation of the Press

Napoleonic normalization, or the Authorities' long drawn-out attempt to sort out the political mayhem resulting from the aftermath of the Revolution, was a laborious process and obviously had an effect on the press. Napoleon more than anybody else knew how easily the press could influence public opinion. He had deftly shown this as he rose to the height of power. Paolo Murialdi writes in his 'Storia del giornalismo italiano' *"Napoleon marched into Milan on 15 May 1796. In his wake, a plethora of journals blossomed, which is exactly what he wanted. Two days later, he wrote to The Directory. "From here shall spring journals and publications of every type which will inflame Italy. Here, where tensions are highest, restrictions will be lifted on the press"*. For three years in the Italian peninsula, a precarious and short-lived freedom of press shall exist. The Neapolitan revolution of 1799 is the most tragic example. At this point, it becomes important to emphasize the transformation of France's perceived role as a melting point, hotbed, and sounding board for modern ideas, on one hand; and how the European countries reacted to the undergoing French expansionism. While The Bastille, Robespierre and The Thermidor Revolution were relatively unknown to a great majority of people outside of France, under General Napoleon they became much more aware of these events. In his famous Menoirs of Saint Helena, the dethroned Emperor will say to Las Cases: *"ublic opinion is a mysterious and invisible power. Nothing can resist it. There is nothing which is more fickle, vaguer or stronger. Despite being capricious, it is always more true, reasonable and just than we might think"*. Bonaparte never lost sight of this reality. As a scholar and aspiring writer, he never avoided engaging in public debate first hand. Such was his reverence for public opinion.

Furthermore, Napoleon, unlike the Royals who had preceded him on birth right alone, was fully aware of his need for consensus as a tool to validate his own power. It is merit and not bloodline which gives a middle-class ruler credibility. Confident of his ability and shored up by non-military successes, Napoleon wanted his public image to be constantly enhanced by the media of his time. He felt obliged to do it on a daily basis. His crowning as Emperor, along with the symbolism which accompanied it, were instruments which conveyed his absolute superiority. Yet, contradictorily, he somehow managed to remain a man of the people. There was no unfathomable distance between him and the masses as there had been under the Ancien Regime. He walked among the masses, pressed the flesh with humble folk. He always answered their questions readily, decisively and affably. This, however, did not suffice. In order for everyone to get the message, it was necessary to pilot, manipulate, and where necessary, limit the flow of information. This press monopoly came into force on 18 brumaire. In the decade and a half between 1800 and 1814, the press was effectively culled. The number of news sheets in Paris drastically dropped from 70 to a mere 4. He placed his own men within the premises of the few remaining news sheet publishers and gave them the task of thoroughly checking all articles for content. Even the reports of citizens could lead to a newspaper being closed. The reasons for closing a paper were very tenuous indeed. So much so in fact, that sometimes the Emperor had to intervene to curb the zeal of his own executors.

Napoleon's favourite publication was Le Moniteur, as it was virtually a hand out of Imperial propaganda. As might be expected, it contained countless interviews with him and did not spare its lavish praise. As soon as he had successfully brought about his coup d'etat, he surrounded himself by a team of communications experts, who might be known today in modern parlance as spin doctors. Each had their own field of socio-political expertise and endeavoured to keep the remaining post-revolutionary factions, such as the Jacobins and the pro-monarchy movement, happy. Napoleon's reign, as is well known, was characterized by his enduring expansionist aims. This meant that public opinion had to be sated through the most essential means. The Grande Armée dispatches fulfilled this role in his communication strategy.

3.6 Europe, the Continental Blockade, Russia and America

Napoleon's historical figure swings between someone who tried to retrieve and impose a 2,000 year old culture and a visionary who sought to catapult his country into the future. His starting point was a strange one indeed, a revolution which overturned the existing balances and shed doubt on dynastic principles and values. The king was no longer an untouchable, all-powerful figure. This, in turn, led to many people rejecting religion, and consequently, France found itself perpetually at war with various factions at each other's throats. The obvious conclusion to be drawn was that if the situation was to be resolved, strong leadership was required. Not having a monarch as head of state meant that other European states with monarchs were horrified. They feared that this "bourgeois disease" might spread beyond France's boundaries. Such was the zeal and fervour with which the revolution was carried out. This stand-off situation became a trap for Napoleon, who felt that the best way to defend his country against the anti-revolutionary coalition was to attack and expand. He now feels "condemned" to export the spirit and conquests of 1789 beyond France's borders. This ran contrary to his original plans. France was in so much such turmoil that the new rulers wanted to concentrate on domestic issues and put their own house in order. However, the planned expansionism left everything side-lined and in a state of disarray with very weak governance. Emperor Napoleon adopts various cultural motives, styles and fashions from the dim and distant past. Drawing his inspiration from such historical figures as Charles V, Charlemagne and even the Caesars, Napoleon underpins this new imperial style with high-flown speeches, iconography and architecture. His theatre of operations will be Europe, which has failed to quell France's revolutionary spirit, and whose own people seem likely to follow suit, and thus may topple the remaining monarchies in a domino effect. The continent is his for the taking. This is particularly true of the Italian and German speaking areas which are breaking up and are ripe for virtuous French colonization. These territories are in thrall to revolutionary and subsequent Napoleonic principles. He has already won the battle for the hearts and minds of the people.

●

Given the fact that domestic rather than foreign circumstances dictate that he engages in expansionism, as his power is proportionally linked to his military successes, he combines the old with the new, the ancient glory of Rome is incorporated alongside his futuristic vision for Europe. The idea which inspired The Continental Blockade could also be considered revolutionary, even if it will only be partially effective. Its aim was to unite the European states, both France's own satellite ones in addition to its allies, in a political embargo. Noble as this embargo might have seemed, it sprang from the Corsican's desire for revenge against the British following the naval rout of his fleet at Trafalgar. On paper, its aim was to offset British maritime trade dominance by making overland trade impossible for them. In addition to its instrumental value, this measure was dazzlingly ahead of its time. The scholar, Bertrand de Jouvenel, considers it to be the embryo form of the Common Market, later to become the European Community. Once the fallen Emperor was in exile, he insisted on the rightness of his sweeping vision. Europe will find balance and harmony; *"only through the merging and confederation of the great nations"*, *"It will soon shed tears"* for the consequences of dismantling the French Empire, whose existence was *"absolutely necessary"* to guarantee this balance and harmony. Napoleon had always had these lofty and prophetic visions. He used them to add a certain sheen and profound meaning to his actions, thus restoring to them their lost value for future generations. His great ability to foresee future political developments went as far as his prophetic prediction of the future power struggle between America and Russia.

Leaving his prophetic visions aside, if a closer look is taken at the practical consequences of the measures set up by the empire and its presumed allies, it can be understood how the blockade ultimately hastened the great Corsican's demise. Great Britain's total dominance of the seas allowed her to get round the trade embargos. Firstly, she could simply ignore them, knowing that some of France's not so faithful allies would turn a blind eye. Secondly, she could replace old markets with new ones where the obstacles where insurmountable. As far as his image and consensus were concerned, the Napoleon in charge of the Continental Blockade had vastly underrated, as he had so many times before when defining the content and conditions of agreements which his defeated enemies were made to sign, the negative economic effects which these commercial embargos would have on the territories obliged to respect them. Looking at it from this prospective, it is patently clear that the blockade was destined to be a failure. In some countries such as Holland, governed by his brother Louis, there was wild-cat smuggling. This sorry situation led to him to abdicate in 1810. Wherever the blockade was successfully in force, it created discontent arising from economic hardship. Tensions were high, and the situation was ripe for revolt due to the people's exasperation. Anti-French sentiment grew by the day. This was the last thing the Emperor needed. A big coalition was preparing to wage war against him, so he did not need further hotbeds of tension.

Furthermore, it was the continental blockade which led Bonaparte to make certain decisions which would ultimately bring about his downfall. The invasion of Spain and Portugal in 1807 and 1808 arose from Napoleon's stubborn will to turn into reality a measure which, so far, had displayed too many shortcomings. This campaign, however, will only serve to create a further hostile front to the West of Bonaparte's empire. There was no turning back, the dye had been cast. Napoleon would continue to pursue this cause, however due to a lack of respect towards it, he would continue stubbornly and find himself ensnared in the Russian Campaign a few years later.

~

4

A RITE FOR MODERNITY

*Celebrations, weddings, summits, relationships with Popes and Emperors
are all pieces of a jigsaw which will fall into place to ordain the new leaders*

4.1 The Reintroduction of the Gregorian Calendar
and the Sterilization of the Bastille

*"I would like peace to coincide with the reintroduction of the Gregorian calendar
in the hope that it will bring as much happiness to my realm as it did to the former
one"*. Writing to his foreign Minister Tallyrand on Christmas Day, Napoleon
underlined his desire for the settlement of the Austrian conflict, symbolically
linking it to the retrieval of the ancient tradition of marking the passing of time.
The repression of the Republican calendar was an absolute necessity, given that
it cut France off from the rest of Europe. What counted for Napoleon was his
desire to leave behind him the symbolism of the Revolution. This was achieved,
once he had set up social and institutional frameworks which would stand the
test of time. Under Bonaparte, the bourgeois dictatorship replaced the monarchy of divine right. Even as First Consul, Napoleon claimed the right to appoint
his successor. It was a return to the past, but it did not totally wipe out what had
been achieved in the decade following 18 Brumaire. In writing to Tallyrand, his
behaviour is totally different from that of Louis XVI. The most striking example
was the Civil Code which had come into force a little more than a year earlier
on 21 March 1804. This legislature definitively upheld certain inroads brought
about by the Revolution. It upheld principles such as equality and the respect
for private property. Furthermore, it scrapped feudal privileges connected to
the Ancien Regime and laid down the basis for the modern legal system which
subsequently spread to the rest of Western Europe. Bonaparte himself was fully aware of the importance of this legislature, and it was soon renamed the
Napoleonic Code. When recounting his memoirs to Emmanuel de Las Cases

on Saint Helena, Napoleon underlined the fact that his code bore much more historic value than all his battles put together. The Emperor, with his usual extraordinary awareness, also realized that there was a desire for normalization sweeping across wide swathes of the new ruling French class, and that it would be futile to totally dismantle the radically innovative changes brought about in the wake of the taking of the Bastille. He believed, however, that these profound transformations should be incorporated within a different framework and be given over to rights, procedures and new forms of power. To put all this on track, it was necessary to end this period of transition and to do away with anything which might stoke up yet again the flames of uncertainty and precariousness which had haunted the French during this long period of turmoil.

The reintroduction of the Gregorian calendar contained a hidden message of reassurance. It symbolically doused the flames of Jacobin madness. The era of the mob was effectively over. There was no more space for the rogues who had stormed the Bastille. So, the very same celebration on 14 July had been shorn of any Republican symbolism even before Napoleon was crowned Emperor. The refined rituals which had moved from the streets to the salons were more in line with a monarchy. This was the Prime Consul's aim from the very outset, centralization of power and the wiping out of Republican forms and institutions.

4.2 The Crowning by the Pope as an act of Assertion

The reintroduction of traditional rituals during Napoleon's reign always swung ambiguously between a semiological re-affirmation of the values of the past and the exhaltation of a glorious new era. Napoleon's meteoric rise from revolutionary soldier to life First Consul, then onto his coronation as Emperor by the Senate on 18 May 1804, was a relentless and irresistible one, thanks to his amazing astuteness in gauging modern times. He was a man just like anybody else, yet at the same time, he was superior to everybody. Citizen Napoleon rose to the ultimate rank; that of Emperor. To mark the occasion of this historical turning point, he programmed a sumptuous coronation ceremony at Notre Dame cathedral. On the day, 2 December, the old medieval link between Emperor and Pope was brought back to life with magnificent pomp and ceremony. The Pope's task consisted in merely anointing the already-crowned emperor.
His Eminence had been reduced to the role of a mere bystander, bearing no more importance to anybody else officiating at the ceremony. This show revolved

around one single man. Napoleon then went on to carry out what the Pope did not have the authority to do. He places the crown upon the head of his consort, Joséphine de Beauharnais. It was this very act which was captured on canvas for posterity by the imperial painter, Jacques Louis David. With her head bent forward, Josephine kneels before the royal Emperor, who is also Pope for the day, as he regally brandishes the sceptre of power. The picture is entitled: "The Consecration of the Emperor Napoleon and the Coronation of Empress Joséphine", however what it really portrays is Joséphine's entry to the highest ranks of power. What is important to Napoleon on this special day is the concept of an Imperial Family. He deliberately wishes not to be the sole protagonist inside Notre Dame. It is a painting which now carries more historic weight than the actual event. It is a breathtaking work as it is nine meters thirty one centimetres wide and six meters ten centimetres high. In order to complete this masterpiece, David was granted the luxury of a very special artistic studio, the ancient College de Cluny, founded in 1261 by the monastic Cluny movement, and closed down during the French Revolution. Due to monetary squabbles and the Emperor's complex demands and requirements, David took a lifetime to complete it. In order to commemorate a ceremony which had been attended by thousands of French citizens, people were invited to the Emperor's favourite painter's studio to act as models. There were even rumours, somewhat similar to today's tabloid gossip, that Josephine had an excessive role in the development of the masterpiece, thus causing friction within the walls of David's studio.

⁂

What Napoleon really wanted was for this masterpiece to portray the new bourgeois-imperial dominance of which he had set himself up as the leading light. The fact that it did not portray events as they really were held no importance for him. One glaring incongruity in the picture is that it shows his mother Letizia as being present at the ceremony, when in reality she had been delayed on her journey and had not been able to attend her son's greatest moment. The Emperor finally managed to see the masterpiece at the beginning of 1808 and was pleased with it. It took a further two years before this colossal portrait was put on public view. Only a few months later, this inspired work of David, which had cost him so much time and toil, was unceremoniously shifted to his private studio and removed from public view. Many things had changed, the most important of these was that Napoleon had decided to abandon Josephine and now had his heart set on marrying Maria Louise of Austria.

4.3 The Spanish Campaign in contrast
to the Tilsit and Erfurt peace treaties

Napoleon is also modern in as much as he was fully aware of how many potential communication opportunities could be gleaned from the careful setting up
of an event. The summit at Tilsit in 1807, which followed the aftermath of the
battles of Eylau and Friedland, both of which were won by the French Army but
they had come at a terrible cost in terms of the toll of soldiers lost, was an act
of political realism. The French Emperor knows fully well that his new Russian
enemies, unlike the Prussians and the Austrians, have virtually a full strength
army. Knowing a potential clash could be just as damaging as it is unacceptable, Napoleon, from the privileged winning position, grabs the opportunity
to show his magnanimity and respect towards the strength and person of Tsar
Alexander. At Tilsit, France and Russia seek to split Europe into two spheres of
influence in a renewed spirit of brotherhood. Napoleon, in conciliatory mode,
looks to find in Alexander, a blood-line emperor and the most powerful of the
age, further confirmation of the legitimacy of his bourgeois power.
His power springs from his military prowess and political leadership of France
in the aftermath of a bloody revolution.

The choice of a truce, an agreement and of mutual recognition, are all exploited to the hilt to further enhance Bonaparte's public image. The new entente
with Alexander, who just a few months earlier had labelled his new French ally
a usurper, must receive adequate public coverage. This requirement was met
by the setting up of a summit, rich in symbolism, aboard a sumptuous raft in
the middle of the river Niemen. All the other European leaders, starting from
Fredrick Wilhelm of Prussia, were expressly excluded. The message is patently
clear: Napoleon, the enemy of half of Europe, having defeated the fourth anti-French coalition, is now in a position of strength and is willing to deal with
one former enemy who he considers to be his only equal.
On this occasion, as on many others, Napoleon chooses to deal directly with
his enemies. When there is conflict or friction, he prefers to avoid third-party
mediation, as he is convinced that points of convergence over reasons and demands can only be reached when face-to-face with the adversary. This hands-
on communicative approach by a leader in order to resolve conflict has recently
been adopted by the leading schools of project management.
The consistency of the results achieved, which could probably be put down to a
resounding error of judgement on Bonaparte's part, is a totally different matter.

Although Napoleon might have appeared to be magnanimous in asking nothing but Russia's participation in The Continental blockade, it was never going to bear fruit over the long term, given the parlous state in which Russia found itself. At the time of the Tilsit summit, by the Tsar's own admission, the Russian army was a shambles, having barely any rifles. The trust which Napoleon placed in Alexander led Stendhal to state in his Life of Napoleon: *"He was never cut out for politics. Every time he picked up the pen, he undid what he had achieved with the sword"*. How could he be blamed for making such an attempt at an alliance? This is borne out several days later in Milan, when the Emperor had a frank exchange with Melzi, the Italian politician. According to Stendhal, Melzi had informed him, *"that Russia had an abundance of raw materials yet had no manufacturing industry whatsoever. Therefore it would be very unlikely that the Tsar would honour an agreement that would only wreak economic havoc, both on him and the aristocratic classes"*.

-◆

Regardless of its short-term successes, there is no doubt, according to historian David Chandler, that Tilsit constitutes "the prototype economic summit". It was an event which combined reserved political protocol with a thirst for absolute power. Napoleon and Alexander's sorties on horseback go beyond the bounds of politics and would suggest they were soul mates in achieving the same goal. Whilst on the subject of soul mates, or Elective Affinities, it was Goethe himself, the father of the German language and author of the aforementioned work, who would play a part in the life of Napoleon, when the second summit between the Emperor and the Tsar was held in Erfurt. Napoleon expressed his desire to meet both the writer-poet alongside his kindred spirit, Wieland, at the so-called "Congress of Princes" held in the Eastern German town.

In the meantime however, the political landscape has changed dramatically. Napoleon has completely misjudged the political climate and has committed a basic error. This will have a negative effect on his future manoeuvres and, to a lesser extent, will hasten his downfall. His thirst for power will lead to his personal interests overshadowing his interest for France. By doing so, he neglects the very principle on which he has built his success; consensus.

The French Revolution and its ideals, along with the heroic victories of the Napoleonic army spanning the end of the eighteenth century and the beginning of the nineteenth century had won over the hearts and minds of the Spanish people. King Charles IV's popularity had waned dramatically due to his perceived weakness, and Prime Minister Manuel Godoy had become the effective leader of the country. Relations between France and Spain were cordial to such an extent that Napoleon and his army had frequently crossed the border into Spain without any complaints or opposition from the locals.

The situation changed when Napoleon, taking advantage of the fact that he had to send troops to Portugal given his lack of confidence in the ruling Braganza family's ability and desire to uphold the Continental Blockade against the British, began to set up permanent garrisons on Spanish soil.

The Spanish people had had enough of Charles IV's indolence and gave their support to his son Ferdinand, Prince of Asturias, who, for some time, had been openly hostile to his father. On 18 March, the rebels stormed the Royal palace of Aranjuez and proclaimed Ferdinand VII as the new King of Spain.

It is at this point that Napoleon's insatiable thirst for power blinds him as to the restraints of sensible government in delicate situations where a sense of balance is required. Instead of waiting for the turbulent situation to settle down and consequently lending a hand in bringing about liberation alongside the native revolutionary forces, as the French armies had done previously, Bonaparte choose instead to take advantage of the weakness of the newly-installed regime. The mendacious Statute of Bayonne, was nothing more than a confidence trick which led to the abdication of Ferninand VII in favour of Napoleon's brother, then to the former's imprisonment. The choice of his own brother marked the end of any form of solidarity between the Spanish people and the tyrant's army from the other side of The Pyrenees.

Given his fatal political error, the time between the summits of Tilsit and Erfurt had carved an enormous negative cleft in the political landscape for Napoleon. At Erfurt, he had to get his message across as effectively as possible. He had no other choice. Sandwiched between the Spanish crisis and the threat of the Austrians declaring war on him, he had to play for time. His main concern was to quell the Spanish revolt and then, to a lesser extent, he had to hold off an attack on his eastern front. In order to do both, he needed Alexander's support and endorsement, even more than he had done at Tilsit.

He will obtain little more from the Tsar than a reaffirmation of what was agreed in the former German town, which was later handed over to Russia at the end of the Second World War. Meagre as this reaffirmation was, it served to give him an immediate boost in popularity. Sumptuous events such as balls, theatre shows, hunting parties, military parades and religious ceremonies were organized to celebrate this perceived success. All these events serve to enhance the meeting of the great rulers in Erfurt, called the "Congress of Princes", as might be expected. At the end of the day, once again, it all revolved around the Emperors of France and Russia.

History will relentlessly run its course. Between the meetings in Tilsit and Erfurt, the Tsar had the opportunity to carefully weigh up the flattery lavished on him by the Corsican which, at the time, had seemed so noble and generous after the defeat at Friedland. The Tsar, having carefully considered the facts, had come to the conclusion that he was dealing with an unreliable ally whose ambitions ran counter to both European stability and to his weary and exhausted people, including the economically productive middle classes. All that remains of Erfurt is its stately magnificence which served Napoleon much more than any of the other participants.

5

THE GLORIOUS DEFEAT

*How his "Memoir of Saint Helena" acted as a springboard
to transform a defeated man into a posthumous legend*

5.1 The Exception of Waterloo

As far as Napoleon is concerned, the famous saying could be paraphrased as: *"He who lives by communication, dies by communication"*. Communication, or rather lack of it, as it turned out, was a major factor in bringing about his downfall. For once, he failed to get his message across and suffered a humiliating defeat.
Most of the blame does not lie with Napoleon himself, but rather with one of his most trusted soldiers, Emmanuel de Grouchy, Marshall of France, who in the past had led the 'holy battalion', the imperial bodyguard made up solely of officials. While Napoleon was in exile on Elba, de Grouchy gave his services to the new Bourbon regime. When Bonaparte came back to power, he did not discipline his Marshall as he had done with many others. On the other hand, the Emperor had little room for manoeuvre. Despite having a vast army numbering roughly two hundred thousand men, over the course of his various battles, he had lost many leading generals. Having been left with a small élite group of expert soldiers, he now had to make do with many rawer and less experienced troops, compared to those he had had at his disposal in the golden age of Austerlitz and Jena. Between 1813 and 1815, his fallen veterans could only be replaced with ardent yet untrained young conscripts known as marie-louise.

There is no doubt that this sweeping change within the ranks of his troops was one of the major factors which brought about his downfall. However, de Grouchy's behaviour on the battlefield did not help matters either. The French Marshall had set his sights on chasing down the Prussian army led by general Gebhard Von Blücher. The latter had been defeated at Ligny on 16 June 1815, but not to such an extent as to be seriously demobilized. De Grouchy gravely mis-judged the enemy manoeuvres and set about chasing down his own deserters rather than the Prussian enemy. This course of action took him towards Liége, while Von Blücher's men had gone North. De Grouchy's fatal and unforgivable error was that he did not head to Waterloo with his cavalry division in order to give reinforcements to Napoleon. Waterloo is exactly where Von Blücher head-ed, which proved fortuitous and was instrumental in sealing the outcome of the battle. Grouchy's behaviour defies logic. Even without receiving any dispatch-es requesting help from the Emperor, he should have followed the golden rule of warfare prevalent at that time and headed towards the roar of the cannons. Grouchy simply did not act and failed and hence he failed to reach either of the essential objectives, firstly, the definitive surrender of the Prussian army and secondly, providing his Emperor with reinforcements. It did not turn out to be a total betrayal. After Waterloo, the Marshall displayed great courage and military know-how in facing up to and defeating the enemy in order to clear the way for the troops' return to Paris. Napoleon's surrender left Grouchy no other alterna-tive than to go into exile. He only returned from the United States in 1831 after officially being pardoned.

The debacle of Waterloo was brought about by the shortcomings of a communi-cations system which had in the past always proven to be the jewel in the crown of the French army, thanks to the efficiency and rapidity with which communi-cation flowed. In short, there had been a communications breakdown and the smooth-running machine had for once failed to do its job. Basic codes of Na-poleonic warfare had not been respected (such as heading towards the roar of the cannons). There is no doubt that this formerly infallible system had caused Napoleon to labour under the illusion that help was surely on its way. Unfor-tunately and disastrously for him, it never did. To reiterate, it was undoubtedly the breakdown in the communications system which proved to be the decisive factor in the French defeat. Other negative factors obviously play their part as well. As mentioned previously, the troops were a lot less experienced than their predecessors. Another anomaly was the line formation of the French soldiers. Rather than being broken up into columns which flanked one another, they were set out in one long line. This meant that his front-line was perilously narrow, consisting of only a few hundred men. This turned them into easy cannon fod-der for the enemy who systematically scythed them down line by line.
The majority of historians agree on that fact that even if Napoleon had been victorious, his star was already on the wane and he would only have postponed

his inevitable decline. Regardless of this, the errors committed on 18 June 1815, both military and communicative, certainly hastened the great Corsican's decline.

5.2 Best Seller Ante Litteram

Julien Sorel's "Holy Book", the unforgettable hero of Stendhal's: "The Red and The Black", has become a touchstone to quote and underline whenever scholars wish to discuss the foundations of nineteenth century romanticism. Sorel's "Scriptures" consist of Rousseau's "Confessions", alongside Napoleon's official army dispatches and "The Memoirs of Saint Helena". This great novel appeared a mere fifteen years after Napoleon's death. The Emperor has become a legend despite the British having tried to sully and tarnish his image with their constant flow of negative propaganda. How did it come about that a defeated emperor who had been demoted to his former role of general and sent into exile on a far-flung island between the Atlantic and the Pacific, and who is no longer treated with respect and deference by those he talks to (very often he had no audience at all), namely his jailer the British governor of the island Hudson Lowe, would manage to regain worldwide respect and esteem?

Undoubtedly, it was the book: "Memoirs of Saint Helena", written by the Count Las Cases, which help to tip the balance in his favour. The real star of the book is certainly not the author, a mild and unassuming nobleman with a sharp business sense. As always, it is Napoleon. Once again, thanks to his usual lucidity, he grabs the tool made available to him and exploits it to the full. The fact that it was Las Cases rather than other writers specialising in Napoleon who scored a bulls eye and that his book, "Memoirs of Saint Helena", became a Best Seller ante litteram being one of the most reprinted books of the nineteenth century, thus allowing its author to live off the publishing rights, counts for very little. It is significant that the adage: "It is the winners who write history", proved absolutely wrong in Bonaparte's case. In the wake of Las Cases' literary success, there was a boom in books and articles examining and giving in-depth analysis of Napoleon's glory years rather than ones concentrating on his final days and rapid decline. Napoleon's non-religious side stirred up a lot of interest. That all this could happen comes down to our hero's ingenious intuition. The dethroned Emperor's extraordinary awareness allowed him to exploit and transmit his message to a wide audience by giving his own personal slant on all he had lived through and experienced throughout his glory years.

All these ideas came to him while on Saint Helena and not before. During his previous exile on Elba, he had been equally wracked by doubts and had even considered taking his own life; a sombre thought which he would also consider during his second exile. He felt certain, however, that he could escape from Elba and leave behind the bleak destiny his enemies had imposed on him. Whilst in exile on Elba he underwent a different dilemma. This splendid theatre of enforced idleness brought up desires and emotions from his young manhood. His youth had been compromised by the duties arising from having to govern and maintain order in a great but turbulent nation. The power which he had grasped with his own hands was an instrument for dominating entire peoples and armies, yet at the same time it had overwhelmed him. Life on this Mediterranean island brought him back in full contact with nature and filled him with peace and tranquillity. The experience was similar to the one which he had had during his boyhood on his native island of Corsica, the one which had enthused his soul with Revolutionary ideals.

₰

It is in Bonaparte's early youth that the roots of his burning desire to permanently act are to be found. The roots in question are ones regarding a nation's desperate needs to heal gaping social wounds which would then be ripped open during the Revolution. To Napoleon's mind, many of the leading figures from that time had acquired a renown which was vastly overrated both in terms of good and evil. According to Bonaparte, it was wrong to associate Robespierre as the leading exponent of The Terror. The fact that the most gruesome phase of The Revolution came to an end depended on the circumstances rather than other people's inability to perpetuate the momentum of radical ideology. One factor in particular, public opinion, ensured that the terrorists and their doctrine would die after the demise of Robespierre, due simply to the fact that the people were tired of excessive revolutionary zeal. The Corsican had an interesting metaphoric image of public opinion. The Memoirs of Saint Helena inform us that he envisaged it as an invisible mystery power which nobody or nothing could resist. Stating things thus, Napoleon gives the clearest ever example of where his destiny lays. This master of public opinion ultimately became its victim. The military leader seemed to have the same relationship with the masses as Socrates had with his daemon or voice of conscious. The fact that he was so in tune with the Zeitgeist, and was able to expertly interpret the implicit demands of the people, led him to abandon the hopes and dreams of his youth and to thus take on the mantle of Supreme Leader. On Elba, with his life's trajectory virtually at an end, he lives and re-embraces, for a short time, those youthful dreams which had turned into regrets. However, his inner voice pushes him yet again to take action, by once more taking up the mantle of the champion of a lost generation which is condemned to dedicate its existence to restoring a social and political balance previously knocked out of kilter by the masses who stormed the Bastille. Furthermore, the subsequent disorder following in its aftermath up to 1793 and beyond had to be cleared up. For the French citizens of his age and for the new ruling classes, or more precisely, those who have the capability of shaping the new stages in French history, it is not possible to enjoy neither the fruits of victory nor the newly consolidated social frameworks. It is like living in a whirlpool, where public opinion is like an erratic compass which is constantly swinging from regicide to restoration.

The idea of trying one more time to thwart the return of the Ancien Regime, thus to ensure that all the battles and conquests won over fifteen years would not come to nought, were all factors which drove the Emperor to take up arms once again. A further factor in pushing him into action might have been the crushing idleness and boredom of the golden cage in which he found himself on Elba. Some more cynical people might just put it down to vanity and personal ambition, given his behaviour in the past and the ensuing results.
On Saint Helena, however, the possibilities for "taking action" are zero. He feels as though he has been tricked by the British and that France rather than himself, has been gravely offended, and yet he is isolated in the middle of nowhere on the other side of the world and cannot do anything about it. He plays his last card. His escape will not be physical, rather he will metaphorically evade his prison and achieve victory by communicating with future generations.

5.3 L'histoire c'est Moi

With "Memoirs of Saint Helena", Napoleon becomes his own personal historian. This approach is as unique as it is efficient. A totally different historical slant and reading, in complete contrast to the one which had been given by the newly-restored aristocratic families who had returned to power after Waterloo, emerges from Las Cases' work. The self-effacing author of "Memoirs", who considers himself as a mere mouthpiece, often does not seem to be up to the task of grasping and conveying the weight and scope of the former Emperor's musings and considerations. What he does convey, however, is the equally brilliant and overwhelming personality of his subject. The complete contrast between the enforced idleness of the island and the frenetic action-packed life he had led before arriving there, result in sharpening Napoleon's perception of the past and in facilitating his breaking it down into key events. *"He talks about these events as if they had happened hundreds of years ago. His language effectively places them in the distant past"* observes Las Cases. On some occasions, it is Bonaparte himself who underlines this fact. One example of this is when he remembers his mistrust towards those who describe the strengths and weaknesses of others to him. He reassures his chronicler about the diversity in the relationship which binds them together. *"Here, my dear man, none of these dangers exist. We are from another world. It is as though we were chatting whilst strolling along The Champs Elysés. You have no ulterior motive and I do not feel mistrust".*

It is his remoteness, both physical and metaphorical, which conditions Napoleon's burning urge to renew his image for future generations. Being the great strategist that he is, he realizes that, although his physical imperial power and grandeur, alongside his command of the Grande Armée have irreversibly waned, he still has the chance to impose his image on the collective imagination of future generations. With this in mind, Bonaparte sets about to dismantle the negative propaganda spread through the writings of the enemies who have defeated him. *"So what could I be attacked for, and on what basis could an historian defend me? For my intentions? This indeed would be my best defence. For my despotism? The historian could show that dictatorship was absolutely necessary given the circumstances. Will I be accused of having placed restraints on freedom? The historian could point out that society was riddled with unruliness, anarchy and mayhem. Will I be accused of being a cruel warmonger? He could point out that it was always I that was attacked first. Will I be accused of imposing universal monarchy? He will be able to attest that events at the time randomly brought this about, in addition to my enemies slowly but surely forcing me into doing so. Finally, I will be asked whether it was because of my ambition. I admit that I was full of ambition, but it was of the most well-meaning and noble kind. What I aimed to do was to establish and even sanctify the empire of reason, and bring about total fruition of the human faculties!"* The Emperor's musing are not mere high-flown rhetoric, especially when he refers to effective commitments which objectively influenced politics and behaviour while he was at the height of his powers. There is a certain one-sidedness to his arguments when he alludes to the fact that the bringing about of freedom, equality and social progress, which he flaunted both in France, across Europe and even in Egypt, were in no way linked to his own volition or his personal ambitions. Furthermore, he conveniently overlooks the sometimes cynical exploitation of universal ideals in order to serve the motherland, as occurred when drawing up the Treaty of Campoformio. In his "Memoirs", Napoleon attempts to become the chaste and pure champion of the revolution by airbrushing out his pragmatic and cynical manoeuvring. Against all odds, he mostly manages to pull it off! Julien Sorel is an outstanding example of how successful Bonaparte was in reinventing himself. Once Las Cases' book had been put in circulation, it had a stirring effect on many young men and intellectuals who were disappointed at the failure of the impossible dream. Napoleon has now become the embodiment of the death of this dream and this is precisely the reason why, due to so much unrest and disillusion, so many hotbeds of revolt spring up all over Europe. The people refuse to give up on the impossible dream. They still want to believe in heroism and the rediscovery of the individual. Despite it having failed once, they still believe that reason is the only weapon for human and social progress. They are therefore once again ready to take up battle in its name.

One thing for which Bonaparte should be praised was his farsightedness in realizing how the anti-revolutionary coalition's endeavours to return to the previous *status quo*, in which the *élite* dominated, would be short-lived. Simply put, there could be no return to the past. The ideals of the revolution would continue to smoulder under the ashes of its funeral pyre.

This smouldering was the springboard for "Operation Memoirs", which aimed to resuscitate a myth which was effectively dead and buried. This time round, he had the additional advantage of written form which could embellish the myth, thus giving it a sheen that had never really existed. Naturally, not everybody took the bait. It was none other than Stendhal, an acute observer of the realities of his time, who pointed out Bonaparte's duplicity. In writing his "Life of Napoleon", he endeavours to de-construct the excuses which Napoleon used, having become First Consul, to justify the transformation of the Republican regime into a dictatorship. *"It was never Napoleon's intention to grant the French people as much freedom as they needed and then gradually increase it as the various opposing factions died out and public opinion had calmed down and become more reasonable. He never attempted to assess just how much power could be handed over to the people without them abusing it. He tried, instead, to figure out the minimum amount of power with which they would be happy. The Constitution, which he gave to the French people, was calculated (if we can use the word calculated) to reduce this wonderful country to a state of absolute monarchy, rather than to make them aware of freedom. All Napoleon could see was a crown, and he allowed himself to be dazzled by this threadbare and anachronistic toy. Had he so wished, he could have set up either a Republic or a two-chamber government. However, his only ambition was to found a new monastic dynasty".*

Stendhal provides a refined paraphrasing of what Napoleon's own brother, Lucien, had stated as a seventeen-year-old. Writing to his older brother Joseph, he describes Napoleon thus, *"I have discovered in him (…) an ambition which is not selfish in the real meaning of the word, but which goes beyond his love for the public good. In a free state, he is definitely a dangerous man. I have the impression that his character tends to tyranny. Should he become king, I fear he would be a tyrant and his name would conjure up horror both for our fellow citizens and for the generations to come".* Emil Ludwig quotes this letter in his biography of Napoleon, underlining the fact that Lucien's prophecy stems from the competitive sibling rivalry he felt towards his elder brother. As an adolescent, Lucien would never have imagined in his wildest dreams that several years later, it would be he himself who would pave the way for his elder brother to set up the Consulate, then the dictatorship.

5.4 The Champion who Brought the Different Peoples Together

"The truth is that I have never been the master of my own actions. I have never completely been myself. I did have my own plans, but I was not able to carry some of them out". These are more startling confessions contained in "The Memoirs" of Las Cases. Further, Bonaparte states: "I governed according to circumstances". By saying this, he is not trying to exculpate himself. The former Emperor is now resigned to the fact that he has nothing left but to restore his tarnished image. He is therefore committing himself to ensuring his military defeat will not wipe out all he achieved during his fifteen years of glory.
"Napoleon is reiterating the fact that flexibility and an ability to adapt to situations is an asset, and that it would have been sheer madness to force events to fit in with my system. I preferred to adapt my system according to how events developed".
He admits that he was in full control of the situation at certain times by saying: "A man is only a man: *"A man is only a man. The means he has at his disposal*

are futile if he is not favoured by circumstances and opinion". He is therefore displaying his full awareness of the inevitability of certain events. Napoleon is the first to point out that a combination of incredibly lucky circumstances enabled him to reach the very heights of power. In the same fashion, at the very height of his golden age, he underlines the fact that he is obliged to win the consensus of public opinion, as it is the only true source of legitimising his power. It could be clearly seen how wars were a condemnation for Napoleon, as he was constantly obliged to defend himself both from internal and external enemies within the boundaries of an ever increasing empire.

There are clear signs of regret in his above admission. Regrets regarding how much he could have done, had he not been impeded by the prevailing political climate of the time. What is not in doubt however, is that this man was and remains to be a great communicator. At the very height of his rise to power, he was fully aware of the relationship which existed between obtaining the peoples' consensus, which represented the legitimacy of his power, and the defence of revolutionary conquest. He therefore transformed concepts such as the "battle of annihilation" and the "home front" into uplifting slogans, thus inviting and obliging the French nation to politically, economically, and militarily uphold the "Foreign Front", namely their fellow citizens engaged abroad in battle. On the other hand, even in distant exile and ignominious defeat, he continued to send out his messages, which he deemed suitable to the «context of events», from Saint Helena. He declared himself as an advocate for unifying different peoples, Italians, Spanish, Germans and so on. This ideal was never carried out consistently. In reality, the Napoleonic regime merely treated conquered territories either as breadbaskets for France (Italy), or imposed heavy taxes to boost the French state's coffers.

Nevertheless, Napoleon's communicative ability contributed to decorously framing the myth through great swathes of Europe after his death, both under the banner of Republican ideals and new shibboleths such as national awareness. In his sermon to future generations made through Las Cases, Napoleon wanted to put himself across as the standard-bearer of a great turn of events which would give a voice to the different peoples of Europe. His great communicative abilities are perfectly captured in this book, which was put into circulation a mere two years after his death. It will go on to inspire and enflame young idealists against the climate of political conservatism which came about following The Congress of Vienna. The defeated Emperor had always had a paternalistic and manipulative vision of the representation of collective interests. This had to filter down from him and therefore he took great interest in what the people had to say when he went for his walkabouts amongst the masses. He endeavoured to portray himself as one of them, while at the same time, he attempted to read and satisfy the prevailing moods. When dictating his memoirs on Saint Helena, Napoleon shows how important it is for him to be remembered positively by future generations: *"I am not a tyrant"*, he underlines, *"rather the initiator of an irreversible movement for a project of change. It has come to a temporary standstill due to people who have sidelined it".*

⁂

His exile on Saint Helena is a form of martyrdom. It will have a cathartic effect as it will serve to rehabilitate him in the eyes of historians and future generations. He has no hesitation in using a bold comparison. *"If Jesus Christ had not died on the cross, he would not be God. It was his suffering which captured people's minds. If I were not here but rather in America, like my brother Joseph, nobody would think about me and my cause would be lost".* He is portraying himself as the leading light who will change the course of history. As if he were Prometheus, he has snatched the gift of fire from the Gods and given it to France. These "Memoirs", as well as serving to remind present and future generations of his person and his extraordinary deeds, will also serve to reignite nationalistic pride, which will culminate in the acclamations of the people in front of the dead Emperor's remains when they were returned to Paris 1840.

The art of exploiting his defeat to gain popularity will reach its apex through Las Cases' book. Although it is his best attempt, it is not the first. Another notable example is the way in which he overturned his disastrous Egyptian campaign to portray himself as a bearer of culture, alongside the insolent shamelessness with which he informed the French people in dispatch 29 that, "the Emperor was in good health", after the humiliating rout by the Russians. Another startling example is his speech at Fontainebleau to the old guard before he is sent into exile on Elba. He manages to communicate the inevitability of the separation, his usefulness regarding patriotic ends and the temporariness of the detachment. Serving France will be: *"... my only thought and will be the object of all my endeavours".* He is asking his audience not to pity him as he will *"strive to survive and dedicate myself to your glory".*

5.5 The Legend

After his death on Saint Helena, the myth became a legend. Two factors contributed to Napoleon being reinstated as a paragon of virtue; the sterile political climate which brought about a retrograde return to The Restoration, coupled with a grave financial slump in 1815 which was felt throughout Europe. Napoleon's renewed positive image cannot just be restricted to that of the champion of Romanticism. This is just one of the paradoxical consequences resulting from the publication of Las Cases' work and the dictator's death: the advocate of Neo-classicism was lauded by a cultural movement which was the polar opposite in terms of strategy and actions. The phenomenon has a snowball effect and becomes much more wide-ranging. It sweeps across the lower classes, mainly amongst the peasants who feel the full force of the recession and nostalgically hark back to the better times of the not-too-distant past, which they perceive as much better. These are the people who knew relative prosperity thanks to being called upon to feed the soldiers of La Grande Armée. During the Napoleonic years both under the Consulate and the Empire, they experienced a steady rise in income. The peasants' urban equivalents, which will soon be labelled "the Proletariat", also shared the same positive sentiments towards Bonaparte. His popularity is best summed up in this sort of lullaby written by Berenger, a rough translation of which is: *"Although he might have harmed us, the people still adore him, How they adore him. Granny tell us about him. Tell us about him".*

This is the complete opposite of the negative "Boney" propaganda rife on the other side of The Channel. While French grandmothers sing their praises of Napoleon, who is seen as nothing more than a monster by their British counterparts, the former Emperor will also receive more stately and poetical tributes. Examples of these are "The Fifth of May" by Manzoni, an epic poem dedicated to him by the Austrian Grillparzer, in addition to further literary tributes from such great writers as Puskin and Heinrich Heine. It is patently clear from these attestations that the wind is blowing favorably for the defunct Emperor. Events have a snowball effect and seal the stages of the meteoric rise of his legend. The Arc de Triomphe is inaugurated in 1836 and is dedicated to the revolutionary armies and the Empire. Four years later, he will again make his mark, posthumously, as the forerunner of the stage-management and communication techniques which he had patiently developed in the previous century. He is long since gone, but his giant figure overshadows everything in the ceremony which takes place on 15 December 1840. His ashes are brought back from Saint Helena to Les Invalides. Heine describes it thus *"All of a sudden on a cold winter morning, he is once again amongst us. On a triumphant hearse bearing the marks of his illustrious victories, his remains make their way through the early-morning mists. As if by magic, these mists dissolve once the cortége has reached Les Champs Elysées. The sun fends through the clouds and, for the last time ever, kisses its favourite son whilst dazzling magnificently against the golden imperial eagles at the front of the cortège"*.

If the Second Empire in France decisively boosted officializing the myth of ceremonial rites in public works, in addition to cultural and artistic expression, in Italy, newly established ties with its transalpine neighbour fostered a somewhat forced rediscovery of Napoleon. During his speech on 15 August 1859 in the courtyard of Brera Palace, on the occasion of the unveiling of a statue of Napoleon which had been hidden in the basement of the very same building for several decades, Giulio Carcano goes as far as saying that Napoleon should be considered the trail-blazer of the road which leads to national self-determination, and thus should provide inspiration for what was happening in Italy at that very time. Carcano, however, conveniently forgets to mention the Treaty of Campoformio. What matters at this stage is Napoleon III's support for the Italian War of Independence, hence a blind eye is turned to the treachery of his predecessor. In reality, there has already been a partial rehabilitation of the figure of Bonaparte, and this is not only in Manzoni's epic poem. It is also present in the most famous work of the great Italian patriot, Silvio Pellico, who expresses his internal anguish and suffering within the confines of Spielberg prison, by comparing it to what Napoleon went through on Saint Helena and using it as a springboard for creating a dialogue. Pellico genuinely believed that Napoleon was too great, a figure to be consigned to the dustbin of history as a disillusioned patriot. *"He who brought tears to our homeland and who I do not like, I now beg to be presen"*. Pellico does not like him at all, yet is so in thrall to his legendary status, that he wishes his spirit would visit him in his prison to pass onto him the moral support and strength he had shown during his own exile. Here, Napoleon is transformed into a romantic hero, despite the resentment for the destiny to which he has condemned Italy through his previous actions.

⁂

There are two versions of Napoleon which came about after his downfall. The first one was the godlike and all-conquering patriot, while the second one was the defeated demonic tyrant. It will be undoubtedly the more positive one which will stand the test of time. The most important factor which keeps the myth alive is Bonaparte's great skill of self-promotion, a prototype marketing genius. His cause was consolidated and given momentum by the publishing of Las Cases' book which keeps the flame burning for future generations. No marketing campaign, however, will last in time and stand up to the weight of history unless it is adequately updated.

NAPOLEON
*A REAL VECTOR FOR CULTURAL,
ECONOMIC AND SOCIAL DEVELOPMENT*

by Charles Bonaparte
*(President of The European Federation of Napoleonic Cities
and eldest of the last living branch of the Bonaparte family)*

As Roberto Race explains, apart from being a great statesman and an unrivalled leader, Napoleon was also an early adopter of modern communication and marketing techniques.

Waterloo, the conflict of conflicts, the most famous battle in history, is commonly associated with its loser rather than with its winner. Waterloo is remembered by many as the battle Napoleon lost, not the battle Wellington won. In collective memory, Napoleon's defeat is almost eclipsed by the grandeur of his character, and is glorified through images, literature and other representations. As Race underlines, Bonaparte displayed an ability to control his own image and predict its impact on different people, from the French masses to his enemies, beyond borders and to the generals he fought against. His completely unique ability to strategize and use technical advances were ahead of his time.

Race provides several examples in his book, without resorting to pure anecdotes. "Napoleon the Communicator" tackles a fascinating theme in a tone that is simultaneously rigorous and revelatory; whilst also being scientific tinted with a hint of fantasy. The book's underlying thesis is explored within the different dimensions of Napoleon's titanic figure: starting from the military tactics he used to his manipulation of the iconography that represented him, the crowds surrounding him, his use of culture to create his own dimension as a pre-Nietzschean superhuman, along with his manipulation of information. The book also tackles his extraordinary concluding performance; the story of himself handed down for posterity within the memorial of Saint Helena, a collection of his memories written by Emmanuel de Las Cases. The way in which Race's book revives this subject represents one of the most concrete and enjoyable ways to rediscover the roots of modernity in one of the all-time legends of history. This is exactly the reason why Napoleon is an interesting tool for the territorial marketing of cities and territories associated with the European Federation of Napoleonic Cities.

The Federation

Above and beyond our opinions on the man and his actions, as elected officials of the Napoleonic cities, we understand the importance of the moral and material heritage bequeathed to us. We understand how much Napoleon's life work has influenced our cities – not only their history, urbanism and fortunes, whether good or bad; but also their present situation. It is therefore our desire to promote this heritage in order to continue creating meaning and wealth for our people, and thus better prepare them for the future. This desire stems from our understanding that with sound knowledge and a fair appreciation of our cities' history, our fellow citizens will be better equipped to face the challenges of modern times. The Federation was created to unify the different threads of our Napoleonic history on one common page. We are all the richer for our differences, and for each of our cities, Napoleon might have been a builder, a legislator, an administrator, a conqueror, or a vanquished enemy. Sometimes, he would have been all of these in turn.

The result is a panoply of sharply contrasting attitudes towards Napoleon, perfectly illustrating the richness and complexity of his labours, thus forming a rousing embodiment of contemporary culture. It is said that Napoleon is the most famous historical character in the world, and that new books are written about him each and every day. Societal progress is not at all linear, however Napoleon succeeded in writing a new page of history, this putting an end to the Ancien Régime and its privileges to lay the foundations for a new era – an era of freedom and equality. This is very much how we have come to understand the man today. Born under the Ancien Régime and raised during the Revolution, Napoleon was a man capable of laying the foundations – those famous 'masses of granite' – for a new Republican era.

Though his government's structure and methods still harked back to former times, and though he systematically resorted to war to resolve conflicts, Napoleon's reforms were clearly oriented toward the future. He was able to modernise France and much of Europe with far greater success than anyone before him, leaving in his army's wake the Napoleonic Code, the Concordat of 1801, the Cadastre, the abolition of privileges, and an end of serfdom. Thus, Napoleon literally and figuratively marked out new boundaries.

Our federation has been working on a European scale since it was recognized as a European Cultural Route by the Council of Europe. On this level, Napoleon's heritage is a powerful lever for the development of European territories. The interest and curiosity aroused by the hero, as well as his reputation, can be used as a basis for cultural and historical tourism, for the projects concerning living and heritage culture, as vectors for the creation of wealth and thus jobs.

We have launched a dozen local projects throughout Europe. They aim at unifying cities, regions, cultural institutions and companies on a common page in Napoleon's history, or a particular European area, for instance Napoleon's childhood and education in Corsica and in the Mediterranean region, his government in Paris and imperial palaces, military campaigns in Italy, in Central Europe, Spain or Russia, the creation of modern Poland, and many other subjects that are dealt with on a local level, according to the perception of Napoleon's role in the region. Our actions allow to mobilize resources from European programmes in order to complement national, regional or cities' resources.

European companies are also interested in our actions. Among such companies, one can find not only those which are connected directly or indirectly with tourism or culture (one of the most dynamic sectors of modern economy), but also those who wish to benefit from the incredible renown of Napoleon's name, a world-wide known hero in our globalized culture. He is Google's second most searched for historical figure.

NAPOLEON
THE MESSAGE FORCE

by Mario Rodriguez
(Political consultant. Professor in Communication)

Reading about one of the greatest ever historical figures from a modern perspective helps us to understand the world as it is now.

When I saw that Roberto Race had lined Napoleon up alongside the communications industry, my initial reaction was that he had simply been lured by a fad. Furthermore, I thought that he was a latecomer to this fad, as there had been a tidal wave of works dedicated to this topic, namely the effect of the link between marketing and Italian politics.

However, this book gives a much deeper analysis, and provides us with insight into the times and social situation in which we now find ourselves. It shows us how the roots for today were established centuries before, and explains our modern day political situation.

So what has remained unchanged in time? We can detect a constant pattern in all political events and this is especially true for Napoleon Bonaparte's case. He can be considered the prototype leader, the one who came in from outside of the established political caste and subsequently broke the mould. He was a man who led by deeds and got his message across without the help of mass media.

For someone like myself who does not merely focus on the present but also the past when considering the impact of communications on human events, Roberto Race's book acts as a sort of sieve, which allows the reader to select the constant principals of behaviour which will lead to success. One principal stands out from amongst the others, namely the ability to consciously govern the communicative aspect of one's behaviour, whilst considering the relationship between the communicative abilities inherent within our personal system of relations and the way we communicate outwardly, as the glue which holds society together and creates a sense of unity. In short, a sweeping vision and aware-

invented the telegraph, the radio, the TV, the telephone, the internet and the smart phone, we have led ourselves to believe that we also invented political communication. However, this is not the case. Slowly but surely, we have rediscovered, recognized and become aware of the role and importance of one of the many fields of life known as politics. Communication, therefore, has come to be defined as the ability or skill possessed by a person, be they aware or unaware of it, to create dialogue and transmit meaning or a sense of purpose to the masses. It is a system through which meaning may be transferred through the generation of feeling. As often happens, we wonder how we did not figure this out much earlier, as it all seems so obvious and consistent. Above all, we ask ourselves how come there are still so many people who have not figured it out for themselves.

-●

These reflections, however, take nothing away from the power of new devices and technologies and their ability to characterize eras and ways of life. In their turn, they create new meanings, interpretations and representations. By reflecting on Napoleon, his life and his deeds, and taking a fresh look at how he got his ideas and meanings across, we are able to see communication in a new light; it is different, more mature and long lasting. It allows us to remove the clutter amassed in the field of political communication created by the mass media, with television being the main culprit. Due to a number of important reasons, including significant descriptive yet not exhaustive results, political communication has specifically concentrated on social mechanisms inherent in the relationships existing between various media systems. When speaking of political communication, we refer to its evolution from mass media to social networks, along with its transformation into firstly infotainment, then politainment, and consequently into institutional political systems.

This "simplification" was useful at a time when the influence of television was on the rise in the field of media. Nevertheless, this process of simplification failed to provide a convincing solution to the core issue *"the symbolic construction of authority and the relationship of trust, both of which bond leaders and followers and act as a "social glue" (Elster 1995)", that "consist of meticulous calculations and worthy ideas leading to the development of affective ties".* (Panebianco 2009). After a quarter of a century spent reflecting on this observation, certain questions regarding the role and importance of communication in the field of politics still remain unanswered. On the other hand, there

ness are required to ensure that everything holds together and runs smoothly. Napoleon is the master of this. He never fails to get his message across, being fully aware of the ensuing consequences of his actions. He is also able to meet his targets and achieve the desired results. His is an effective, well-oiled, and smooth-running communications machine which achieves results.

Napoleon comes to embody the "Zeitgeist" in terms of communication, which at the time was in its infancy. He was able to effectively exploit whatever he had at his disposal. He is fully aware of the power of these new instruments such as the press, in addition to more traditional eye-catchers connected to pomp and ceremony, such as the grand parade. He also has a keen unprejudiced attitude towards other innovative media, the most obvious example being David's giant oil paintings. Another of his winning cards is his eye for detail, which is encapsulated in the way he and his other general wore an immaculate eye-catching uniform. He was ahead of his time and foreshadowed the modern day concepts of look, location, posters and even mass televised events.

This book's strength lies in the way it underlines that, to govern with awareness requires leaders to deftly use the lever of communication, and this has been a constant throughout history.

From the viewpoint of those who deal in political communication, Roberto Race's book is a useful tool for both communication professionals and scholars to further consider the power of communication within the fields of TV and social networks, along with their relevant marketing techniques: consideration regarding Napoleon the Communicator underlines the fact that politics entails communicative action and gives it meaning, both in reality as well as symbolically and creatively. This has always been the case. Techniques change over time, but the basic core of meaning remains.

꠸

The third Industrial Revolution, which is an 'information technology" revolution, coupled with inroads made in neuro-science (alongside less technological factors such as the 20th century philosophy of linguistic turns of phrase), have allowed us to develop our awareness towards the importance of communication. This is actually a rediscovery rather than a new invention. Misguided by a constant torrent of technological innovations and an ever increasing number of objects at our disposal, we have been led to believe that political communication was strictly linked to devices and techniques. Therefore, just as we

has been an increase in doubt due to the onslaught of cognitive psychology and neuro-science.

In my opinion, there is no way getting around from it. It can, therefore, only be of great advantage to look further back in time to Napoleon Bonaparte and his deeds to obtain a new and positive view on the above present-day conundrum. It is necessary to focus our attention on the actual structure of meanings which political specialists consciously use to influence public opinion. This is important as it would enable us to liberate political communication as a set of symbolic values from within the repressive confines of its devices and transmission techniques. In other words, we are talking about "the cultural contexts which influence attitudes and shape lives". Geertz said: *"We must open the dictionary of description and cultural analysis in order to add new concepts to it". He went on to add, however: "Unfortunately, nowadays, political theory either limits itself to synoptically listing threadbare principles which will undergo Manichean death throes, or it will be reduced into an ideological struggle in the form of forced deductions derived from cast iron premises. Political theory is still not up to the task of defining the unruliness which characterizes our modern era".*

The above historical consideration is in tune with the modern one expressed by Roberto Race regarding Napoleon, which allows us to focus our attention on the lucid and purposive communicative actions of political players, in addition to the mindful and savvy use of communication.
This communication, which is of a cultural, ritualistic, and symbolic nature (best defined with the words: 'endless game' and 'permanent campaign') cannot be contained within the limits of subsidiary and transmissive approaches.
What stands out in the Emperor's commitment to historical reconstruction, is the way he pays careful attention to the tiny building blocks of macro-phenomena when using the levers of communication. Napoleon's story is the sum total of all his communicative actions, of the operative decisions he took upon himself and of the visions which were the lynch-pin of his everyday life and behaviour.

*

I was particularly impressed by this constant search for micro-foundations of macro-phenomena, because as Angelo Panebianco contends, *"Political Science research reaches better results when it adopts a commensurate theory for both the player and the actions. In this way, it defines the relationship between the player and*

the institutional context in which he finds himself and builds bridges to deal with the transition mechanisms between micro-interaction and macro-phenomena".
Finally, it is important to add that Roberto Race's new slant on reviewing Napoleon the Communicator's life and actions dovetails perfectly with new mythologies that have sprung up in modern times, and are for the most part linked to Americanization. The most obvious ones which come to mind are political consultant and spin doctor, but there are many other illusions and delusions that are linked to the so-called political marketing.

Hence, what lessons can be drawn if we take into consideration the importance Napoleon assigned to his words, his exemplary behaviour, his relationship with his followers, which we have often labelled as an "Americanization" of politics, along with the inevitable impact on carrying out politics as a consequence of new techniques and devices? We always do the same things but we use new instruments to do them. This is the big difference which should not be underrated. Instead, lessons should be learnt from them and subsequently metabolized into our behaviour. It is only with hindsight when we mull over them and recount them that we have done the right thing in the right way.

~

FROM HIS OWN MOUTH

*Some of his sayings and maxims which have help to bolster
the myth of Napoleon Bonaparte*

The Great leader's continual war

"Either we beat them or they beat us"

"Inevitable wars are just wars"

"A commander should never allow the victors or the defeated to rest"

*"A general who does not pay attention to his soldiers'
needs does not deserve to lead them"*

"True men are hard to find"

*"He who fights against his homeland is like a son who
wants to kill his mother"*

"Special circumstances call for special solutions"

"He who believes in rules is lacking in genius"

"Rules lead to mediocrity"

"There is no strength without wit"

*"The best soldier is not the one who fights
but the one who marches forward"*

*"Nothing can be considered done,
while there still remains more to be done"*

"War is cruel for the people and terrible for the vanquished"

"Danger is at its height at the moment of victory"

"He who is afraid of losing glory, will surely lose it"

"It would be better never to have lived than to live without glory"

"We must laugh at men to avoid crying for them"

*"Men have mutated from their natural state.
They have become cowardly vile worms"*

"Woe betide the general who arrives on the battlefield with a battle plan!"

*"At the beginning of a campaign, it is important to consider whether
or not to move forward; but when one has taken the offensive,
it is necessary to maintain it to the last extremity"*

"Directing military action is only half of a general's work"
*"One of the most important things is establishing
and ensuring communication"*

"We walk faster when we walk alone"

"True wisdom lies in firm determination"

Doing things by half results in total loss"

Regarding the Revolution and its conquests

*Revolutions wreak instantaneous destruction
but take a long time to rebuild the future"*

*"A revolution is an opinion which makes itself heard through bayonets.
Revolutions can be compared to stinking manure which brings
about the growth of beautiful vegetables"*

"Golden rule: revolutions and terror go hand in hand"

*"In times of revolution, a soldier should never despair
of anything when he has courage and perseverance"*

*""In revolutions, there are two types of people: those
who carry them out and those who take advantage of them"*

"Freedom and equality are two magic words"

"The people's sovereignty is unalienable"

Hovering between transparency and ambiguity

"It is much better to have sworn enemies than deceitful friends"

"Whether something is a virtue or a vice depends on the circumstances"

"The strongest do not negotiate, they dictate conditions and are obeyed"

"Either I give an order or I keep my mouth shut"

"*The best way to keep one's word is to not give it*"

"*There is no worse condition than that of a people
which has to submit to another*"

"*Arms should never be taken up for vainglorious
ambition or the thirst for conquest*"

"*For he who founds an empire, men are not men,
rather they are mere instruments*"

Men are what you want them to be"

"*Men have a heart, laws do not*"

"*The sovereignty of the people is an illusion invented by our ideologues,
listless democrats and impotent republicans*"

"*My policy is to govern men as the majority wishes.
This is, I do believe, the best way of recognizing the people's sovereignty*"

"*A general must be a storyteller*"

"*Men are more easily ruled by concentrating on
their vices rather than their virtues*"

"*Historical truth is a conventional fairy-tale*"

"*Men's desires are not as excessive as is believed*"

"*Making men happy is much easier than one might think*"

"*Those who can no longer be rewarded must be made to fall into disgrace*"

Measuring himself against public opinion

"*It is the consensus of the masses which gives an opinion sovereignty*"

"*I want to establish civil order in France. So far there have
only been two powers, military and ecclesiastic*"

"*Rulers must make themselves feared and respected*"

The people's love is nothing but esteem and respect"

"*The French nation recognizes in a flash those who work for
her and those who are against her. Her sentiments must always be spoken to,
otherwise her restless spirit gnaws at her, quivers then explodes*"

"*It is necessary that law and the government treat everybody fairly
and equally. Rewards and honours should only be bestowed
upon those whom the people think worthy of them*"

*"I did not inherit the crown from my forefathers,
it was the will of the nation that bestowed it on me"*

"What counts is the common man's opinion"
"We are made to direct public opinion, not to talk about it"

"Good politics consists in deceiving the people into thinking they are free"

His views on education and culture

*There can never be a stable political state until we have
a body of teachers preaching fixed political principles"*

*The spirit is enhanced by being nourished with different types of food.
A vast variety of reading pleases the imagination just
as a vast variety of sounds pleases the ear"*

*"The only conquests which do not leave the
soul embittered are those which conquer ignorance"*

"Equality must be the first foundation of young people's education"

""Public education is the primary responsibility of the government"

*""All citizens should contribute to state security. Obedience
should not spring neither from ignorance nor from stupidity"*

How he saw women

*"Catherine II was a woman born to command
and was fully worthy of a beard on her chin"*

"A statesman should never bring a woman into his cabinet"

"A woman's role in times of trouble is to soothe our woes"

"Love should be a pleasure, not a torture"

Reforms and social progress

"Military courage and civilian courage are like chalk and cheese"

"Divorce is a law which suits a couple's interests"

*"Nothing runs more contrary to the institution
of the family than a divided one"*

Talking about himself

"We must speak to the eyes to persuade the people"
"I will be the Brutus of kings and the Caesar of the Republic"

"It reads like a novel but it is my life!"

"Destiny has been stronger than me"

"I love power like a musician loves their instrument. I love it as it allows me to create sounds, arrangements and harmonies"

"My great talent which sets me apart from others is the ability to see everything clearly"

"I have carried the weight of the world on my shoulders and in doing so have been left weary"

"A general's presence is indispensable. He is the head, he is the army It was not the Roman Army which conquered Gaul but Caesar. It was not the Carthaginian army which brought fear to the very gates of Rome but Hannibal"

"The superior man is impassive. He ploughs on regardless, impervious both to praise and criticism".

~

CHRONOLOGY

15 august 1769: He is born in Ajaccio, Corsica.

15 May 1779: He enters the Military Academy of Brenne, where he will stay for 5 years.

30 October 1784: He is appointed Sub-lieutenant. He leaves Brenne for the Champs de Mars Military Academy in Paris.

14 July 1789: The Bastille is taken. Napoleon goes back to Corsica the following September.

1790: Initially attracted to the Corsican Independence leader Pasquale Poli, he then distances himself having realized the former is a mere megalomaniac

21 January 1793: Luigi XVI is beheaded on the guillotine.

11 June 1793: He returns to France with his entire family to flee Paoli and his reprisals as Paoli has now targeted him as an enemy due to his position in the French National Guard.

8 July 1793: He settles in Nice where he leads a modest life.

31 July 1793: A short 20 page work of his in published in the Le Courrier d'Avignon. It carries the title "Le souper de Beucaire", and it features a dialogue between four people, one of whom convinces the others of the worthiness of The Republican Cause. He has it printed at it own cost and it brings him some fleeting glory.

12 September 1793: Napoleon ends up in Toulon where he is appointed colonel and is given the task of defending this garrison town against the British siege.

28July 1794: Robespierre is executed on the guillotine.

9 August 1794: Napoleon is arrested on suspicion of having plotted to help Robespierre. Once the accusations prove groundless, he is released ten days later.

5 October 1795: Appointed to rank of deputy leader of The Home Guard by Barras, he successfully quells a royalist insurrection in Paris.

2 March 1796: Appointed commander of the Italian Expeditionary Army.

9 March 1796: Marries Josephine Beauharnais.

12 April 1796: Routs the Austrian army led by General Beaulieu at Cairo Montenotte.

10 May 1796: Napoleon beats the Austrians once again at Lodi. This opens the way to march on Lombardy. He fights at his soldiers' side and earns their veneration. Five days later, the French Army triumphantly marches into Milan.

5 August 1796: Napoleon beats the Austrians (led by Field Marshal Wurmser) yet again at Castiglione

8 September 1796: History repeats yet again as he defeats the Austrians at Bassano.

17 November 1796: The magnificent victory at Arcole, which will be captured on canvas.

14 January 1797: A further victory over the Austrians this time at Rivoli. Four days later, the French Army triumphantly march into nearby Verona.

2 February 1797: Mantua also falls to him and his army after a long siege.

19 February 1797: The Peace of Tolentino: Pio VI gives up Avignon and Venassin County over to France while, Bologna, Ferrara and Romagna are given to the Cisalpine Republic.

March 1797: An intense military campaign resumes against the Austria. The French take Gradisca then on 21st Tarvisio, and Bolzano on the 22nd; Generale Bernadotte marches into Trieste, Generale Joubert marches into Bressanone. Il 27 Generale Massena occupies Villach on the 27th and follows up by occupying Klagenfurt on the 28th.

May 1797: Napoleon overturns the aristocratic government of Venice and replaces it with a Democratic Republic which is sympathetic to France.

29 June 1797: The Cisalpine Republic comes into being.

17 October 1797: Treaty of Campoformio. Venice is given over to Austria. All territory on the left bank of The Rhine as far up as Cologne is given over to France and Lombardy becomes part of the Cisalpine Republic.

5 December 1797: Napoleon triumphantly returns to Paris. The command of The Italian Expeditionary Force is given over to General Berthier.

11 February 1798: Berthier occupies Rome and proclaims The Roman Republic.

19 May 1798: The Egyptian Campaign begins. Napoleon embarks from Toulon for Egypt. His army is made up of roughly 35 thousand men who travel on 200 ships. Their principal aim is to break British naval dominance of the Mediterranean and take control of "The Routes to India"

9 June 1798: The French Fleet occupies Malta. After 250 years, The Knights of St John lose their grip on the island.

1-2 July 1798: Landing in Egypt and the conquest of Alexandria.

21 July 1798: Great victory over the Mameluchs at The Pyramids. Three days later, Napoleon marches into Cairo.

1° August 1798: The British Fleet led by Lord Nelson annihilate their French counterpart in the Bay of Abukir.

27 November 1798: The army of Ferdinand IV King of Naples marches into Rome and chases out the French soldiers. Under the leadership of General Championnet, the French troops will recapture Rome a few days later and re-establish The Roman Republic.

29 December 1798: Great Britain, Russia and the Kingdom of Naples line up together in the second so-called anti-French coalition.

23 January 1799: The French general Championnet marches into Naples and on 26th The Neapolitan Republic is proclaimed.

15 February 1799: Expansion from Egypt to Syria, the French army defeat the Turkish Army at El-Arich.

7 March 1799: Napoleon takes Jaifa. The citizens will be massacred in the siege and this will be followed by an outbreak of plague.

12 March 1799: The Directory declares war on Austria.

19 March 1799: Napoleon begins the siege of St John of Acre, an iconic town from the times of The Crusades.

15 April 1799: French troops abandon Naples.

29 April 1799: The Russians led by General Suvurov defeat the French and occupy Milan.

17 May 1799: After two months of fruitless assaults, Napoleon abandons his attempt to take St John of Acre by siege.

26 May 1799: The Russians march into Turin and restore the kingdom.

10 July 1799: Ferdinand IV successfully retakes Naples. This marks the definitive end of The Neapolitan Republic.

25 July 1799: Napoleone routs the Turks at Abukir.

23 August 1799: He decides to return to France. He boards the ship Muiron and leaves General Kleber in charge of the Egyptian Expeditionary Force.

29 September 1799: The Neapolitan Army retakes Rome which marks the end pof The Roman Republic.

9 October 1799: Napoleon lands in the Bay of Saint Raphael. A few days later, he will reach Paris.

9 November 1799: It is the 18 brumaire on the Revolutionary Calendar and Napoleon carries out a coup d'état. He dismantles The Directory and takes power by setting up The Consulate alongside Sieyès and Ducos.

12 December 1799: The New Constitution is tabled. Napoleon takes on the supreme role of First Consul. Two days later the New Constitution comes into force.

7 February 1800: The Consulate is approved by the French people by means of a plebiscite.

6 May 1800: Napoleon leaves France to embark on the second Italian Campaign.

May 1800: Second Italian Campaign. Napoleon crosses The St Bernard Pass and takes Aosta, manages to successfully bypass the imposing fortress of Bard, the impregnable stronghold and outpost of the Austro-Piedmontese Army.

2 June 1800: Once more, he triumphantly marches into Milan.

14 June 1800: He defeats the Austrians led by General von Zach at Marengo in one of his most famous victories. However, must of the glory must be attributed to General Desaix who sacrifices his life for the French cause.

15 June 1800: He signs a peace treaty with Austria.

24 December 1800: Royalists try to assassinate the First Consul while he is making his way to the seat of government. A cart is blown up in rue Saint-Nicaise. Twenty two people die but the attack fails to achieve its aim.

9 February 1801: The Treaty of Luneville is stipulated between France, Austria and Russia. It endorses what was agreed at Campoformio. Piedmont and Liguria are given over to France.

16 July 1801: France draws up an agreement with The Catholic Church.

1 August 1801: General Menou, defeated by the British who landed at Abukir, surrenders on the proviso he is repatriated by the British Fleet. The French campaign in Egypt comes to an inglorious end.

26 January 1802: The Cisalpine Republic is renamed The Italian Republic and is presided over by Bonaparte himself.

25 March 1802: Under the conditions of the Treaty of Amiens, Britain is compelled to abandon Malta just as France is made to abandon its ports in the Kingdom of Naples.

4 August 1802: Under the New Constitution, Napoleon becomes life Consul and supreme power over the other two Consuls.

25 February 1803: With the Treaty of Regensburg, Napoleon made all ecclesiastical possessions which had been confiscated from the church available to the various princes whose lands and territory had been lost as a result of the Treaty of Lunesville. This did not please the British as they were concerned with the growing French influence brought about on the continent due to this alliance between Bonaparte and the German princes.

13 March 1803: Great Britain declares the Treaty of Amiens null and void.

16 May 1803: Great Britain decides to blockade all French and Dutch ships. France declares war on Great Britain.

25 May 1803: Preparations are made for a potential invasion of England.

14 February 1804: A royalist plot against Napoleon led by Moreau, Pichegru and Cadoudal is unearthed. The following day General Moreau is placed under arrest.

9 March 1804: A Bourbon nobleman the Duke of Enghien is captured at Ettenheim in the neutral territory of Baden-Wurtenburg

21 March 1804: Despite having no part whatsoever in the plot, the Duke of Enghien is executed. Napoleon will receive bad publicity for this all over Europe. From Berlin to st Petersburg, the first Consul is greeted with opprobium and disdain.

22 March 1804: The Napoleonic Civil Code is finally completed and it contains and consolidates many legal inroads won during the course of The Revolution.

18 May 1804: The Senate proclaims Napoleon as The Emperor of the French people.

1° December 1804: Napoleon marries Josephine di Beauharnais in a religious ceremony at Les Tuileries.

2 December 1804: Coronation ceremony at Notre Dame Cathedral in which he is crowned Emperor in the presence of Pope Pious VII who gives his blessing.

18 May 1805: He is crowned King of Italy in Milan Cathedral.

August 1805: A third coalition is formed against France, consisting of Great Britain, Austria, Russia, Sweden and the Kingdom of Naples.

15 October 1805: Victory at Ulm against the Austrian Army led by General Mack.

21October 1805: The British fleet destroys its Franco-Spanish adversary at Trafalgar. The British admiral Horatio Nelson is killed during the course of the sea battle.

13 November 1805: Napoleon marches into Vienna with his Grande Armée.

2 December 1805: His most crushing victory. He defeats the third coalition at Austerlitz. He meticulously plans his moves beforehand like a master chess player.

26 December 1805: The Treaty of Bratislava. Austria hands over The Veneto, Istria and Dalmatia to the kingdom of Italy, Under French protection the Rhineland Confederation comes into being including Bavaria, Baden, Württemberg and other minor states.

1° January 1806: The Gregorian calendar is reinstated and the revolutionary one is scrapped.

9 January 1806: The French invade the Kingdom of Naples and The Bourbons flee to Sicily.

15 February 1806: Joseph Bonaparte, Napoleon's elder brother is appointed as King of Naples.

5 June 1806: Louis Bonaparte, another of Napoleon's brother's is appointed King of Holland, and so the Dutch state ceases to be a republic.

September 1806: England, Prussia, Russia and Sweden form anti French coalition

14 ottobre 1806: Napoleon defeats the Prussians at Jena. His general Davout also defeats them at Auerstadt, where the commander of the Prussian army the Duke of Brunswick is killed in battle.

27 October 1806: Yet another triumphal entry for Napoleon. This time into Berlin.

21 November 1806: With the decree of Berlin, Napoleon sets the continental Blockasde in motion. This denies the entry of any ship flying the British flag into any port controlled by France.

19 December 1806: The French march into Warsaw. Napoleon is proclaimed as the Liberator who frees Poland from Russian tyranny.

8 February 1807: The Grande Armée win the Battle of Eylan. It proves to be a bloodbath for The Russians but the French also suffer heavy losses.

14 June 1807: A further victory against the Russians at Friedland. However, as Luigi Mascilli Migliorini writes in his biography about Napoleon "The toll of the wounded, the dying and the dead far outweighed the joy of victory.

9 July 1807: A peace treaty is signed after the meeting between Napoleon and Tsar Alexander I at Tilsit.

19 November1807: French troops led by General Junot and backed by Spanish ones invade Portugal.

30 November 1807: Lisbon falls and French troops cross into Spain.

17 March 1808: The Revolt of Aranjuez. The Spanish rise up against all-powerful Prime Minister Manuel Godoy. The French march into Madrid.

19 March 1808: The King of Spain Charles IV abdicates in place of his son Ferdinand. The latter is declared King Ferdinand VII.

20 April 1808: Napoleon meets Charles IV and Ferdinand VII at Bayonne.

5 May 1808: Bonaparte obliges Ferdinand VII to recognize his father Charles IV as legitimate king. The later is replaced, however, by Bonaparte's brother, Joseph.

7 July 1808: Joseph Bonaparte is declared king. This sets the Spanish people in turmoil.

July 1808: With the military backing Sir Arthur Wellesley, later to become The Duke of Wellington. The Spanish rout the French occupiers. Joseph Bonaparte is compelled to flee to Madrid.

1° August 1808: Joachim Murat becomes King of Naples.

27 September 1808: A short-lasting agreement between Napoleon and Alexander I in the German town of Erfurt.

4 December 1808: Napoleon takes direct control of Spanish Campaign. He marches into Madrid and lays the foundations for his brother Joseph's return several days later.

30 December1808: A fifth anti-French coalition comes into being. It consists of Great Britain and The Austrian Empire.

20 April 1809: Napoleon defeats the Austrians at Regensburg. In the same period, his general Davout defeats them at Tengen, Landshut and Eckmühl.

13 May 1809: He marches into Vienna.

17 May 1809: In order to punish Pope Pious VII for not enforcing The Continental Blockade, as The Pope had allowed British ships to moor in Civitavecchia, Napoleon strips him of all temporal powers. In retaliation, the Pope excommunicates Bonaparte.

6 July 1809: He defeats Archduke Charles of Austria at Wagram. General Radet places The Pope under arrest and has him deported to Savona.

15 October 1809: A Peace Treaty with Austria is drawn up at Schönbrunn. Vienna recognizes Joseph Bonaparte as the legitimate King of Spain. Other concessions made by Austria are the ceding of the Grand Duchy of Salzburg to Bavaria and several Polish territories to the Grand Duchy of Warsaw.

18 December 1809: Napoleon divorces Joséphine.

1° March 1810: He marries Marie Louise of Hapsburg, the daughter of Emperor Franz of Austria, by proxy. The marriage will be officially celebrated later in Paris on 1st of April.

1° July 1810: Due to clashes with his brother, Louis Bonaparte steps down from the throne of Holland in favour of his son Napoleon Louis. A few days later, Napoleon will declare the suppression of the kingdom, which will subsequently be annexed to France.

13 December1810: Alexander I violates the Treaty of Tilsit by letting British ships moor in Russian ports.

20 March 1811: Napoleon Francois Joseph Charles, the first son of Napoleon and Marie Louise of Hapsburg is born. His father bestows the title of King of Rome upon him.

15 March 1812: The sixth anti-French coalition consisting of Great Britain, Russia and Sweden comes into being.

9 May 1812: Napoleon leaves Paris to joins the Grande Armée to march against Russia.

24 June 1812: He crosses the river Nieman and the Russian campaign begins.

22 July 1812: Wellington defeats the French at Salamanca and some days later his army marches into Madrid.

8 September 1812: The Grande Armée achieve victories at Borodin and on the Moskova River but the toll in terms of lives lost is immense.

14 September 1812: Napoleon marches into Moscow.

16 September 1812: A huge blaze engulfs Moscow.

19 October1812: Napoleon decides to commence his Army's retreat.

23 October 1812: An attempt at a coup d'état by General Malet proves unsuccessful.

28 November 1812: On their last legs, Napoleon and his army managed to cross the Berezina River.

19 December 1812: Napoleon returns to Paris.

17 March 1813: Frederick William II of Prussia invokes his subjects to free themselves from the French yolk and war is declared.

2 May 1813: Napoleon defeats the joint Prussian-Russian army led by Blücher at Lutzen.

21 May 1813: He rules the sixth anti-French coalition both Bautzen and Wurzen.

21 June 1813: Joseph Bonaparte, after a wave of victories by Wellington in the Peninsular War, is forced to recognize the legitimacy of Frederick of Bourbon's claim to the throne and abandons Spain for good.

12 August 1813: Austria formally joins the sixth anti-French coalition.

26 August 1813: Napoleon wins in a outstanding victory in a pitched battle at Dresden.

16-18 October 1813: He suffers a heavy defeat at Leipzig.

28 March 1814: The beginning of the French Campaign. The Russians and Austrians invade France. Joseph Bonaparte begins negotiations with the sixth coalition regarding the capitulation of Paris.

1° April 1814: Napoleon takes sanctuary at Fontainebleau. The Senate declare him destitute.

12 April 1814: He relinquishes all claims to ruling France and accepts the Island of Elba instead, for which he sets off from Paris on 20 April.

3 May 1814: Louis XVIII enters Paris as king.

4 May 1814: Napoleon arrives on the island of Elba.

29 May 1814: His former wife Josephine of Beauharnais dies,

1 November 1814: The Congress of Vienna opens and the European map is redrawn.

26 February 1815: Napoleon sets off aboard the brig Incostant from Portoferraio and returns to France.

1° March 1815: He sets foot on the French shore at Vallauris in the Bay of St Raphael. This marks the beginning of his so-called *"Hundred Days"*

19 March 1815: He returns to Paris, from where, just a few days earlier, King Louis XVIII has fled.

25 March 1815: Austria, Great Britain, Prussia and Russia form and sign a new pact against France.

3 May 1815: The Austrians defeat Joachim Murat in the battle of Tolentino.

7 June 1815: Ferdinand IV returns to Naples, taking on the title of Ferdinand I of the Two Sicilies.

9 June 1815: The Congress of Vienna reaches its conclusion. Three days later, Napoleon sets of from Paris to Belgium to face the forces of the anti-French coalition.

18 June 1815: He is defeated at Waterloo by Wellington and Von Bülow.

8 July 1815: Louis XVIII returns to Paris.

16 July 1815: Napoleon hands himself over to the British and boards the Bellerophon, which moors in Plymouth in South West England on 23rd July.

9 August 1815: He is subsequently made to board the Northumberland, which sets sail for the island of St Helena.

15 October 1815: Napoleon arrives on St Helena.

5 May 1821: Napoleon dies.

DESTINATION NAPOLEON
*THE VECTOR FOR CULTURAL, ECONOMIC
AND SOCIAL DEVELOPMENT AT THE SCALE OF A CONTINENT*

In May 2015, Destination Napoleon (www.destination-napoleon.eu), the route created by the European Federation of Napoleonic Cities (www.napoleoncities. eu) in dedication of Napoleon Bonaparte, officially became "European Cultural Route of the Council of Europe".

The originality of Destination Napoleon draws its originality and richness from its continental dimension, in addition to its geographical and administrative diversity, and indeed, due to its historical, cultural and patrimonial magnitude.

Today, Destination Napoleon is operative in 13 Countries, spanning from Portugal to Russia, along with more than 60 European Cities influenced by Napoleonic history and a strong scientific community.

To develop a bottom up strategy, 13 local steering committees have been created in 13 different territories. We opted for a territorial structuring intermeshed throughout our European network, however also deeply rooted within the local area.

13 territories, 13 Local Steering Committees:
Germany/Czech Republic, Wallonia, Spain/Portugal, Italy, Poland, Russia/Belarus, Croatia (under construction), Greece (first contact)

In France: North-West + Antwerp, Imperial Cities, Campagne de France 1814, Route Napoleon (100 days), Corsica.

And 11 topics:
1. The Mediterranean, Childhood and formation: Ajaccio, Toulon, Valence;
2. The Italian Campaigns;

3. The major urbanism projects in the North-West of France;

4. The central power: Paris, Saint-Cloud, Fontainebleau, Rueil-Malmaison;

5. Centrale Europe, War and Peace: Austerlitz, Jena, Erfurt, Weimar, Leipzig...;

6. The resurrection of Poland;

7. The campaign of Russia (and Belarus);

8. The first exile: The Route Napoleon, from Portoferraio to Grenoble;

9. Waterloo and the Route Napoleon in Wallonia;

10. Spain and Portugal.

A special strategy will be developed for Egypt and the island of St. Helena (UK).

BIBLIOGRAPHY

(ORIGINAL TITLES IN FRENCH, ENGLISH AND ITALIAN)

J. Bainville; *Napoleon*; Fayard, 1931.

J. Bertaut; *Napoleon. Manuel du chef*; Petite Bibliothèque Payot.

J. Boudon; *Passion Napoleon. Par l'épée et par la plume*; Paris, Textuel, 2004.

J. Boudon; *Napoleon expliqué à mes enfants*; Le Seuil, 2009.

J. Boudon; *Napoleon Bonaparte. Le 1er Empire*; Editions Jean-Paul Gisserot, 2011.

D. G. Chandler; *The Campaigns of Napoleon*; 1973.

S. Cosseron; *Les mensonges de Napoleon*; Perrin.

T. Crow; *L'atelier de David. Emulation et Révolution*; Gallimard, 1997.

E. De Las Cases, *Il memoriale di Sant'Elena, a cura di Luigi Mascilli Migliorini*, Rizzoli, 2004.

A. Dumas; *Napoleone*; Newton, 2004.

S. Englund; *Napoleon: A Political Life,* 2005.

E. Ferrero; *Lezioni Napoleoniche*; Mondadori, 2002.

E. Ferrero; *N*; Einaudi, 2005.

R. Goetz; *1805: Austerlitz*; Greenhill Books, 2005.

A. Grab; *Napoleon and the Transformation of Europe*; Palgrave Macmillan, 2003.

P. Kotler; *Marketing management*; Pearson, 2007.

G. Lefebvre; *Napoleone*; Laterza, 1991.

T. Lentz; *Nouvelle Histoire du Premier Empire I: Napoleon et la conquête de l'Europe (1804-1810)*; Fayard, 2001.

T. Lentz; *La proclamation de l'Empire*; Nouveau Monde, 2002.

T. Lentz; *Le Sacre de Napoleon*; Nouveau Monde Editions, 2003.

T. Lentz; *Nouvelle Histoire du Premier Empire II: L'effondrement du système Napoleonien (1810-1814)*; Fayard, 2004.

T. Lentz; *Napoleon et l'Europe*; Fayard, 2005.

T. Lentz; *Sainte-Hélène, île de Mémoire*; Fayard, 2005.

W.Lippmann; *Public Opinion*; Dover, 1922.

E. Ludwig; *Napoleon*; 1920.

J. Manas; *Napoleon on Project Management; Timeless Lessons in Planning, Execution, and Leadership*; Nelson Business, 2006.

L. Mascilli Migliorini; *Napoleone*; Éditions Perrin, 2004.

L. Mascilli Migliorini; *Il mito dell'eroe*; Guida, 2003

L. Mascilli Migliorini; *Dizionario critico dell'Italia napoleonica*; Utet, 2011.

A. Maurois; *Storia della Francia*; Mondadori, 1953.

P. Miquel; *Austerlitz*; Albin Michel, 2005.

P. Murialdi; *Storia del giornalismo italiano*; Il Mulino, 1996.

G. Parenti; *Napoleone in sala stampa*;Mauro Pagliai Editore, 2009.

A. Perivier; *Napoleon journaliste*; Plon, 1918.

N. Petiteau; *Napoleon de la mythologie à l'histoire*; Seuil, 1999.

A. Pigeard; *Dictionnaire de la Grande Armée*; Tallandier, 2002.

A. Roberts; *Napoleon: A Life*; Viking 2014.

M. Rodriguez; *"Il ritorno della parola: dagli strumenti di marketing all'approccio simbolico rituale" da Comunicazione politica, 1*; il Mulino, 2009.

L. Salvatorelli, *Leggenda e realtà di Napoleone*; De Silva, 1944.

Stendhal; *Vie de Napoleon*; 1876.

A. Suchet; *Napoleon et le management*; Taillandier, 2004.

J. Tulard; *Dictionnaire Napoleon*; Fayard, 1987.

J. Tulard; *Napoleon, proclamations. Ordres du jour. Bulletins de la Grande. Armée*; Union Générale d'éditions, 1975.

J. Tulard; *L'histoire de Napoleon par la peinture*; Belfond, 1991.

J. Tulard; *Napoleon: le pouvoir, la nation*; la légende, 1997.

J. Tulard; *La vita quotidiana in Francia ai tempi di Napoleone*; Mursia, 1984

J. Tulard; *Napoleon - Les grands moments d'un destin*; 2006.

J. Tulard; *Napoleon chef de guerre*; Tallandier, 2012.

J. Tulard; *Le Monde selon Napoleon*; Paris, Tallandier, 2015.

S.Valzania; *Austerlitz. La più grande vittoria di Napoleone*; Mondadori, 2005.

S. Valzania; *Napoleone*; Sellerio, 2011.

S. Valzania; *I dieci errori di Napoleone. Sconfitte, cadute e illusioni dell'uomo che voleva cambiare la storia*; Mondadori, 2012.

S. Woolf; *Napoleon's Integration of Europe*; 1991.

L. C. Wairy; *The Private Life of Napoleon*; 1900.

SITE MAP

Napoleon on the web
La Fondation Napoleon is the leading international institution dedicated to
Napoleonic studies. This should be the first site you go to.
www.napoleon.org

Napoleonica.org is a search engine/archive made up from various resources belonging
to Fondation Napoleon.
www.napoleonica.org

The Institute on Napoleon and the French Revolution of Florida State University is the
only one of its kind in the USA.
www.fsu.edu/napoleon

Napoleon-battles.com is totally given over to the Battle of Waterloo.
www.napoleon-battles.com

Museums
Il Museo Napoleonico in Rome has a collection of works of art and relics connected to Napoleon.
www.museonapoleonico.it

The site of Musées Nationaux Napoleoniens enables the visitor to consult programmes
and activities which take place at Châteaux de Malmaison, Bois-Préau, and the
museums in l'Ile d'Aix and the Maison Bonaparte in Ajaccio.
www.musees-nationaux-napoleoniens.org

Il Marengo Museum, which was reopened in 2010, tells the story of the Italian
campaign of 1800 and the Battle of Marengo.
www.marengomuseum.it

The Residenze Napoleoniche Museums on the island of Elba are dedicated
to his stay on the island.
www.sbappsae-pi.beniculturali.it

Parcours Napoléoniens - Ajaccio
www.parcours-napoleoniens.com/

Associations

La Fédération Européenne des Cités Napoleoniennes forges bonds between the European towns and cities which underwent Napoleonic influence.
www.napoleoncities.eu

Souvenir Napoleonien is one of the leading Napèoleonic associations in Europe
www.souvenirnapoleonien.org

La Société Napoleonienne Internationale (SNI) founded n Canada is one of the most important English speaking associations.
www.societenapoleonienne.com

Il Centro di Studi Napoleonici in Rome is made up of a group of devoted admirers and scholars.
www.studinapoleonici.it

Events

There are countless re-enactments and conventions centering around the myth of Napoleon and the Bonaparte family.

Bonesprit: A rich calendar of events which takes place in Tuscany, Liguria, Sardinia and Corsica.
www.napoleonsites.eu

L'Associazione Tolentino 1815 which jointly organises alongside Tolentino town council a re-enactment in period costume of the famous battle which was fought there between 2 and 3 May 1815, and considered by many to be the first battle of Italian Independence.
www.tolentino815.it

ACKNOWLEDGEMENTS

This book came into being after a long gestation period. I would particularly like to thank Luigi Mascilli Migliorini, the author of one of the most important biographies about Napoleon. I am grateful for his faith in the project from the very beginning nine years ago, and am indebted to him for his support throughout its development. Its development ran parallel to my own growth as a writer and a person.

I have worked on these pages on and off at various times, which has given me the opportunity to reread and rework them at leisure. Regardless of its great central character, this book is greatly influenced by my own personal interests, experience and passions, namely communication and journalism.

Furthermore, I am sure that these leisurely up-datings and reinterpretations, along with Migliorini's much appreciated and precious input, have been fruitful and ensured that the analysis is not slanted from my own professional viewpoint. I also believe that this approach has enhanced my subject matter and has brought out Napoleon's striking modernity. What is most striking is his refinement in setting up strategies and getting his message across to all sections of society, a feat whichh he was able to accomplish without the help of the technology and the tools at our disposal today that have revolutionized the sector.

The Napoleon which I describe in this book, and here I have been helped by the many business people and managers I have had the fortune to meet during the course of my still relatively short career, brings to mind those managers who are able to motivate and involve their staff and make them feel they are playing an active part in the challenges they will have to face together. For Napoleon it was the battlefield, while for business people it is the factory and the market place. In both cases, it is only those who know what it means to be on the front line that can give out orders and make themselves heard. Napoleon, who, in his own inimitable way, due to his ambiguities and contradictions, manages to be both a "dictator" and a standard-bearer of new revolutionary ideas, whilst also being a bearer of certain values which many people complain are often sadly lacking in today's European industrial and political leaders. Napoleon was fully aware of the fact that *"You cannot lead a people without showing them where the future lies".*

I must express my heartfelt thanks to Egea, the publishing company of Milan's Bocconi University, that published the Italian version of the book.

❁

A big thank you also goes out to one of the fathers of Italian journalism Antonio Ghirelli, who I also fondly remember. Antonio fell in love with the idea of Napoleon as a communications guru and was more than willing to help me modify the project by giving me advice on how to make my work as free-flowing and accessible as possible. He had intended to write the foreword to this book, but unfortunately, he is no longer with us.

❁

My final thanks go out to some special friends: To the C.E.O. of Arti Grafiche Boccia and president of Confindustria Vincenzo Boccia, to whom I showed a rough copy of this book. He was favourably impressed and entrusted myself, the task of writing the autobiography of his father Orazio Boccia, founder of the company.

To Raffaele Jerusalmi, CEO of Borsa Italiana and a board member of London Stock Exchange Group, for giving me the opportunity to be part of such a key organisation; one which is involved in attracting capital in Italy from across the world.

To the CEO of ELITE Luca Peyrano, who involved me in the ambitious and visionary project ELITE: the global community that spans 40 countries and the clear vision to provide companies access to capital, skills and network needed to scale up and make a lasting economic impact.

❀

Last but not least, a very special thank you to my parents, to whom I owe everything. They have always been there to support me and left me wanting for nothing. Likewise, a heartfelt thanks to my brother Marco, a trusty companion in this adventure known as life.

~

www.ingramcontent.com/pod-product-compliance
Lightning Source LLC
Chambersburg PA
CBHW021409170526
45164CB00002B/569